The Steve Biko Memorial Lectures

The Steve Biko Memorial Lectures
2000–2008

The Steve Biko Foundation

and

Macmillan

First co-published 2009 by
The Steve Biko Foundation
PO Box 32005
Braamfontein
Johannesburg, 2017

www.sbf.org.za · admin@sbf.org.za

and

Pan Macmillan South Africa
Private Bag X19
Northlands
Johannesburg, 2116

www.panmacmillan.co.za

ISBN: 978-1-77010-1630

Editorial matter and selection © Steve Biko Foundation Trust 2009
Layout and design © Pan Macmillan and Steve Biko Foundation Trust 2009
Text © Individual authors 2009

The Authors have asserted their rights to be identified as the authors of the Lectures.

All rights reserved. No part of this publication may be reproduced, stored in or introduced into a retrieval system, or transmitted, in any form, or by any means (electronic, mechanical, photocopying, recording or otherwise) without the prior written permission of the publisher. Any person who does any unauthorised act in relation to this publication may be liable to criminal prosecution and civil claims for damages.

Proofread by
Juliet Haw

Typeset in Rotis Semi Sans Light by
Printerboyz, East London, South Africa

Cover design by
Printerboyz, East London, South Africa

Printed and bound by Ultra Litho (Pty) Limited

Contents

	Introduction	1
1	*Iph' Indlela*? Finding our Way into the Future Speaker: Prof. Njabulo S Ndebele | Date: 12 September 2000	5
2	Biko's Children Speaker: Prof. Zakes Mda | Date: 12 September 2001	21
3	Fighting Apartheid with Words Speaker: Prof. Chinua Achebe | Date: 12 September 2002	41
4	Recovering our Memory: South Africa in the Black Imagination Speaker: Ngugi wa Thiong'o | Date: 12 September 2003	51
5	Ten Years of Democracy: 1994–2004 Speaker: Former President Nelson Mandela | Date: 10 September 2004	73
6	Citizenship as Stewardship Speaker: Dr Mamphela Ramphele | Date: 12 September 2005	79
7	South Africa: A Scintillating Success Waiting to Happen Speaker: Archbishop Emeritus Desmond Tutu | Date: 26 September 2006	93
8	30th Commemoration of Steve Biko's Death Speaker: Former President Thabo Mbeki | Date: 12 September 2007	101
9	Energising Democracy: Rights and Responsibilities Speaker: Former Minister Trevor Manuel | Date: 11 September 2008	123
	Special Acknowledgements	141

Introduction

The beginning of the end of apartheid, which commenced with the first democratic elections on 27 April 1994, presented the challenge of disbanding the deeply embedded complexes of race. These complexes of black inferiority and white supremacy, reinforced by an oppressive state machinery, are responsible for framing various aspects of South African life, including public discourse. Historically, black opinion was suppressed and white opinion was granted access to more permissive channels of expression.

Since 1994, an admirable trait of the new South Africa has been an expansion of the culture of public discourse. Never before have so many spoken so audibly, on as many public platforms, about the things that are happening in our society. The AIDS pandemic, the arms deal, the formation of new political parties and the political and economic turmoil in Zimbabwe are a few examples from a growing list of issues that are definitive features of the national dialogue.

The development of this interrogative culture has pushed to the rear of public memory the historic reality that only fifteen years ago such probing voices were silenced. Indeed, like Bantu Stephen Biko, many citizens were persecuted not merely for the views they aired but for those they held, or were said to hold. There existed not only a culture of restraint of the freedom of expression, but also of assaulting the freedom of thought.

It is against this background that the Steve Biko Foundation has positioned itself as a catalyst for national reflection and critical inquiry. The Foundation launched the Steve Biko Memorial Lecture in the year 2000, as the flagship of a broader programme, informed by the values that Biko lived and died for: restoring people to their true humanity.

It has been nine years since that cold, wet September evening, on which Professor Njabulo Ndebele delivered the first Steve Biko Memorial Lecture at the University of Cape Town (UCT). Titled, Iph' Indlela:

Finding a Way into the Future, Ndebele's lecture, falling on the sixth anniversary of South Africa's democracy, was a timely introspection on the state of the transformation process. Crafted and delivered with the precision of a true wordsmith, it set a remarkable tone that has come to be associated with the series.

Continuing with the writer's theme the following lecture was delivered by Professor Zakes Mda in 2001. Titled *Biko's Children*, it was an examination of the new cultural landscape and how the current generation of artists have become occupants and architects of new creative spaces.

In 2002 author Professor Chinua Achebe delivered the third annual lecture, *Fighting Apartheid with Words*. During this, Achebe's first visit to South Africa, he paid tribute to the prophetic gift of the writer, and her or his role in African liberation.

Professor Ngugi wa Thiong'o's lecture *Recovering our Memory: South Africa in the Black Imagination* followed in 2003. Ngugi wa Thiong'o articulated the importance of language in defining ourselves as African people and actualising the much sought-after African Renaissance.

Former President Nelson Mandela reflected in the 2004 lecture, *Ten Years of Democracy: 1994–2004*, on the relevance of Biko's legacy to the emerging African Renaissance and the need for a fundamental change in our consciousness (a change for which Biko had created the blueprint decades before.)

The sixth Steve Biko Memorial Lecture was given by Dr Mamphela Ramphele. Titled *Citizenship as Stewardship*, the lecture focused on the link between the enjoyment of rights enshrined in South Africa's Constitution, the challenge of internalising the values from which they flow and creating a culture in which each individual takes personal responsibility for defending and living those ideals.

On 26 September 2006, Archbishop Emeritus Desmond Mpilo Tutu delivered the seventh Steve Biko Memorial Lecture. The lecture served as a national reminder of the importance of guarding against the degeneration of the social values that have underpinned our struggle for freedom and democracy. According to Tutu, but for the persistence of this challenge of moral decay, South Africa is a "scintillating success waiting to happen".

On 12 September 2007, the occasion of the 30th anniversary of Biko's murder in detention, former President Thabo Mbeki summoned us once more to Jameson Hall to deliver the eighth lecture and, "to celebrate the life of Stephen Bantu Biko and to invoke a vision that has, over the years, inspired all freedom-loving South Africans decisively to defeat the monster of apartheid and racism and realise the dream of liberation".

Mbeki's lecture was a momentous political landmark in that it was a celebration of our political victory through an infrequent yet firm embrace across the lines of political parties.

In 2008, in the midst of a deepening economic crisis in South Africa and the international community, former Finance Minister Trevor Manuel delivered the ninth lecture: *Energising Democracy: Rights and Responsibilities*. In his address, Manuel challenged the nation, reminding us that the end of apartheid did not mark the achievement of a democratic dispensation but the beginning of creating one.

Described by Professor Ndebele as a "resuscitative moment" the Steve Biko Memorial Lecture has become an indelible feature on the African calendar – it is broadcast live in South Africa and forty-seven African countries on television through a partnership between the Steve Biko Foundation and the South African Broadcasting Corporation (SABC).

The Foundation is grateful to the inspirational leaders who have honoured our invitations over the years. We also extend our gratitude to the donor institutions that have supported the work of the Foundation, making it possible for us to deliver on our mandate with dependable excellence.

The Foundation is also appreciative of the University of Cape Town, which has been our partner in the lecture series since its inception. The dedication and support of the university has ensured that the lecture has sustained its growth on a year-on-year basis. This is reflected in the patronage the lecture has enjoyed, which extends well beyond the university community into the nation and the African continent.

Lastly, it is to the trustees and staff of the Steve Biko Foundation that one must return, to extend immense gratitude for a job well done. The many hours of sacrifice by the trustees and staff, both current and past, have helped to build the lecture into a showcase for public dialogue. This dedication is premised on the shared belief that this continent needs to build a critical mass of citizens who are at ease with probing the socio-economic and political issues and challenging dominant paradigms.

This publication is the Foundation's modest contribution towards the development of a culture of critical analysis and diversity of thought. It is for all those who relish intellectual inquiry and find compelling the continuum between ideas, citizenship and social action. It is dedicated to the memory of the silenced voices.

Enjoy, share and come back for more!

Nkosinathi Biko
Chief Executive Officer
Steve Biko Foundation

1

Iph' Indlela? Finding our Way into the Future

Speaker: Prof. Njabulo S Ndebele
Date: 12 September 2000

"Like all social processes, the African reawakening is a messy yet creative development, far from being subject to a body of predictive rules and regulations, nor is it reducible to a political programme."

– Njabulo Ndebele

Iph' Indlela? Finding our Way into the Future

I feel so singularly honoured by the Steve Biko Foundation, which invited me to participate in such a special way in this historic event, tonight.

I want to share with you a small story about the origins of my title. A formidable frustration for most writers is what to do with a blank page. It stares at you with silent, intimidating power. To deal with this situation, I decided to put down words at random. Here they are: peasants, foreign policy, the environment, HIV/AIDS, higher education, the media, Zama-Zama, racism, globalisation, Tito Mboweni, culture, the Truth and Reconciliation Commission, black intellectuals, poverty, two nations, xenophobia, Brenda Fassie, penguins, street children, *Thath' amachance, thath' amamillion,* Trevor Manuel, abortion, market forces, crime, size and shape, game parks, identity, African bourgeoisie, witches, taxi wars, the African Renaissance, cities, tribalism, Cosatu, farm murders, the Human Rights Commission, the Northern Province, primary schools, TV, Tim Modise.

After this brief burst of automatic writing, I leaned back to see if I could spot any emergent trends that could suggest a possible title. I stared at the words and found no sustainable connections to hook onto immediately. But, just as I was about to decide that my random collection of words had not helped, I leaned over as a question formed itself without any effort on my part. I wrote: *"Iph' Indlela?"*. I did, indeed, feel lost. I could find no immediate path through this forest of words.

The only thing that was certain was the realisation that the act of writing is a supreme effort at finding your way through immense confusion. It is the act of "finding your way" through a turbulent sea of words. The only thing that sustains you is a daring act of faith. You'll get somewhere. Somehow, I did. Hence this talk.

This experience hit me as a fitting metaphor for what our country is going through. It struck me that through some daring act of faith, we are "finding our way" through a turbulent sea of events. These events are the words which we write down almost randomly on the pages of our future. We work our way forward through a continuous play of random events. At each point along the way, we have to respond to events both anticipated and unanticipated. We remember, for example, how the elections of 27 April 1994, on which we pinned so much hope, threatened to explode each time a series of unexpected obstacles loomed in the way, getting us to sway precariously between deliverance and desolation!

But by the time we got to the elections, we had done some surviving. We survived the hope that flew on the wings of the release of Mandela, and crashed with the assassination of Chris Hani, threatening never to rise again from the harrowing commuter-train killings and Boipatong. At the same time, kwaito flourished. Later, after the elections, art and politics did a delicate dance over AIDS. Mandela had tea with Betsie Verwoerd. PW Botha, facing a black magistrate, wagged his notorious finger more out of habit than conviction in a tired effort to relive the past.

In the Northern Province, many old women were chased away from their homes or burnt to death after being accused of being witches. Elsewhere, initiates began to die in increasing numbers from circumcisions that went horribly wrong. Nelson and Winnie divorced. Members of the new black elite took up membership of the wealth-making class, driven by compelling visions of instant wealth. Some crashes and disappointments occurred as empowerment dreams faded. We were so excited as we formulated new policies to cover every aspect of national life. But we also saw student activism falter and waver, losing its visionary vitality as it strangely began to look like PW Botha's wagging finger. The hearings of the Truth and Reconciliation Commission came, often tearing us apart, and then left, leaving us emotionally drained but still holding on to our faith.

I refer to these events almost randomly in order to convey the very real sense of finding our way through randomness. But I also want to suggest that this is our own peculiar randomness. It prompts a set of responses that incrementally define us. It is impossible to approach randomness from a singular perspective. We look for trends and shifts, and react, sometimes in control, sometimes drifting until we find a foothold that enables us to regain control. It seems to suggest that the way to look for the way is not to focus on specific issues, but rather to look for emerging tendencies which provide an explanatory context which, while not exhaustive, opens up more room for new, innovative solutions. I locate this search in the realm of consciousness: something that Steve Bantu Biko struggled with intensely in his brief but dramatic life.

On 12 September 1977, Steve Biko died in detention. Two days later, the then-Minister of Justice, Jimmy Kruger, is said to have "provoke[d] laughter among delegates to the Transvaal Congress of the governing National Party with remarks about the death. '"I am not glad and I am not sorry about Mr Biko ... He leaves me cold." The Minister also agree[d] with a delegate who applaud[ed] him for allowing the black leader his 'democratic right' to 'starve himself to death'".[1]

Commenting to the press on his verdict after the inquest into Biko's death, presiding Magistrate Prins followed his political leader and declared some three months later: "to me it was just another death. It was a job like any other."[2]

Of course, the cause of death was not starvation. It was "Head Injuries" which led to "extensive brain injury".[3] This leads us to the memory of what must be one of the most imagined of events in South African history – imagined, because only four men witnessed it. Yet, the rest of us, who were deeply affected by the horror of the situation, the outrage it evoked, and the bonds of solidarity and empathy which it strengthened, can still see it vividly in our minds, almost as if we were there in that journey through the night.

I am reminding you of the naked, manacled, and lonely body of Steve

Biko, lying in the back of a Land Rover being driven through the night from Port Elizabeth to a prison hospital in Pretoria, by Captain Siebert. It was a distance of more than 700 miles, which ended in his death.[4] According to SW Kentridge, counsel to the Biko family, Steve "died a miserable and lonely death on a mat on a stone floor in a prison cell".[5]

There is a continuum of indescribable insensitivity and callousness that begins as soon as Steve Biko and Peter Jones are arrested at a roadblock near Grahamstown on 18 August 1977. It starts with lowly police officers who make the arrest in the relative secrecy of a remote setting, and ends with a remarkably public flourish, when a minister of government declares that Biko's death "leaves him cold". This situation lets us deep into the ethical and moral condition of Afrikanerdom, which not only shaped apartheid, but also was itself shaped by it.

It strikes us now just how terribly unreflective Afrikanerdom became once apartheid had wormed its way into the centre of its moral fibre. When apartheid culture became both a private and public condition, defining a cultural sensibility, Afrikanerdom significantly lost much of its sense of irony. In this situation, the combination of political, economic and military power, validated by religious precept, yielded a universal sense of entitlement. Afrikanerdom was entitled to land, air, water, beast, and each and every black body.

At this point, the treatment of black people ceases to be a moral concern. Speaking harshly to a black person; stamping with both feet on the head or chest of a black body; roasting a black body over flames to obliterate evidence of murder (not because murder was wrong, but because it was an irritating embarrassment); dismembering the black body by tying wire round its ankles and dragging it behind a bakkie; whipping black schoolchildren; handing to "an illiterate [black] mother presenting her ailing infant for treatment ... a death certificate in order that the [white] doctor should not be disturbed in the night."[6] when the infant dies: these are things one who is white, in South Africa, can do from time to time to black bodies, in the total scheme of things.

No wonder the death of Steve Biko left the minister cold, and that Magistrate Prins could admit to having just witnessed another ordinary death, just as he would have had another glass of water. In all this, there is a chilling suggestion of gloating which borders dangerously close to depravity. Suddenly, "the heart of darkness" is no longer the exclusive preserve of "blackness"; it seems to have become the very condition of "whiteness" at the southern corner of the African continent. Its expression will take various degrees of manifestation, from the crude to the sophisticated.

That is why such instances of the desecration of the black body have yet to evoke significant expressions of outrage from the former educational, religious, cultural and business leadership of this country, caught in the culture of "whiteness" which they built. Certainly, not to the extent of anything that signals a historic movement towards a new social and moral order. Indeed, the quest for a new white humanity will begin to emerge from a voluntary engagement, by those caught in the culture of whiteness of their own making, with the ethical and moral implications of being situated at the interface between inherited, problematic privilege, on the one hand, and on the other, the blinding sterility at the centre of the "heart of whiteness".

I confess to being one of those who had an ambivalent attitude towards the recent national conference on racism. On the one hand, I welcomed the attention paid to this national problem of racism. On the other hand, I remain deeply worried about the terms on which the problem was highlighted and engaged. I am bothered by the phenomenon of a black majority in power, seeming to reduce itself to the status of complainants as if they had a limited capacity to do anything more significant about the situation at hand than to draw attention to it. It is not that the complaints have no foundation; on the contrary, the foundations are deeply embedded in our history. But I cannot shake off the feeling that the galvanising of concern around racism reflects a vulnerability, which could dangerously resuscitate a familiar psychology of inferiority, precisely at that moment that the black majority ought to provide confident leadership through the government they have elected.

I worry that the complaining may confusingly look like a psychological submission to "whiteness" in the sense of handing over to "whiteness" the power to provide relief. "Please, stop this thing!" seems to be the appeal. "Respect us." I submit that we moved away from this position decisively on 27 April 1994. We cannot go back to it. It should not be so easy to give up a psychological advantage.

I am bothered by the tendency that when a black body is dragged down the road behind a bakkie, we see first proof of racism rather than depravity and murder; as if, if the causal link between racism and murder could not be established, the gruesome killing might not attract as much attention. When we give to racism in Africa this kind of centrality of explanation, we confirm the status of the black body as a mere item of data to be deployed in the grammar of political argument, rather than affirm it as violated humanity. The inherent worth of a black body does not need to be affirmed by the mere proof of white racism against it. The black body is much more than the cruelty to which it is subjected. If we succeed in positioning ourselves as a people, above this kind of cruelty, we deny it equality of status. We can then deal with it as one among many other problems in our society that needs our attention.

I think this is what Steve Biko meant when he cautioned against "the major danger" he saw "facing the black community ... to be so conditioned by the system as to make even our most well-considered resistance to it fit within the system, both in terms of the means and of the goals".[7] It is possible we are not entirely out of this danger.

Is the foregrounding of race and racism a veiled admission that perhaps there is, as yet, no material basis for the black majority to contain this scourge through the imposition of its own versions of the future? Does this speak to the black majority's perception that perhaps they are not yet agents of history?

I ask these questions in the knowledge that white racism in South Africa no longer exists as a formalised structure. We conjure in our minds the continued existence of such a structure to our perceptual peril. There is no evidence of a Ku Klux Klan that is regrouping somewhere in the far-flung corners of the country. On the contrary, with the disintegration of apartheid as a formal structure, white racism has reacted in a number of ways.

In some cases it has simply died. In other cases, particularly where strong pockets of white power remain, such as in commerce, industry and in higher education, it has either mutated and assumed the colour of change while retaining a core of self-interest, or has genuinely struggled with the agonies of embracing necessary change.

In other cases, racism also continues to exist as individualised pathology, frequently exploding into acts of suicide or desperate acts of brutality against black bodies in sight. In almost every case, we witness a crisis of identity with various degrees of intensity. But what these various forms of reaction do show, is the danger inherent in a singular approach.

That is why the black majority carries the historic responsibility to provide, in this situation, decisive and visionary leadership. Either it embraces this responsibility with conviction, or it gives up its leadership through a throwback psychological dependence on racism which has the potential to severely compromise the authority conferred on it by history.

Father Aelred Stubbs writes: "Given the circumstances he faced of a strongly entrenched, powerfully armed minority on the one hand, and a divided, defeated majority on the other, perhaps the political genius of Steve [Biko] lay in concentrating on the creation and diffusion of a new consciousness rather than in the formation of a rigid organisation."[8]

The relationship between emergent social process and organisational forms created to define and assist such social process, is a complex one. A way of life is not reducible to institutional forms designed to support it. Indeed, when the Black People's Convention was established in 1971, there were arguments to the effect that Black Consciousness was a quality of being rather than an organisational project which could be subjected to harassment and banning. In our own day, the African Renaissance as an emergent historic phenomenon, is often used interchangeably with the notion of the African Renaissance as an institution-driven project seemingly designed to midwife the African future. In my view, the latter cannot meaningfully come before the former, although it can anticipate it.

The problem is not so much the establishment of organisational forms, but the threat of constricting rigidity in organisational interpretations of social process. Potential rigidity and ownership of definition can pose a number of threats. I think that despite the wars, the famine, outlaw governments and HIV/AIDS, some reawakening is underway. Some economies are growing.

There is a creeping spread of democracy. The Southern African Development Community (SADC) and other regional economic formations are making a committed effort to contain decay and help along positive trends. Like all social processes, the African reawakening is a messy yet creative development, far from being subject to a body of predictive rules and regulations, nor is it reducible to a political programme. It has yet to be satisfactorily characterised as an irreversible process.

It goes without saying that my approach is to put more stress on emergent phenomena than on evoked realities. I will now explore briefly what I mean.

David Philip Publishers published a remarkable little book earlier this year. It is entitled *Marketing Through Mud and Dust*, by Muzi Kuzwayo. I was fascinated by the central idea behind this book. It is this: "the economic future of this country lies with blacks".[9] A simple but profound statement. What it states cannot be otherwise in a country with our kind of demographic profile and history. From this perspective, this book fundamentally rewrites the textbook of South African marketing.

Kuzwayo tells the story of a township taverner's contact with the "representative" of a certain company. "'Most reps'", says the taverner, "'do a sterling job, but man, I don't know where they get some of them from. You can see that the guy is well educated but is not street smart at all. The problem is that reps are interviewed in an office environment and the human resources people want to see how they fit into the office as opposed to the streets where he'll be marketing the product'".[10] What this suggests is that the pressures of life in the township will significantly influence the strategic choices to be made in company boardrooms and in academic departments and faculties of universities. Such institutions will be responding to the pressures of increasingly dominant social forces, which will over time exercise a decisive hegemonic effect. A situation such as this cannot be led by policy. Policy can only develop from it in order to support it.

Commercial and industrial enterprises, and institutions of higher learning which fail to recognise this fundamental shift in the orientation of the economy, will not survive in the medium to long term. To survive in the future, they will have to rethink and innovate around the needs of the emerging black market. This market, of course, has always been there. But it was rendered officially invisible because the state was primarily constructed around meeting the needs of its white citizens. Clearly, the white market is not big enough to shoulder the burden of economic growth. It can accommodate only so much growth before it begins to run aground and stagnate.

Similarly, there will be an optimum capacity in both economic and cultural terms, beyond which white residential areas can become a home to black people, to any significant degree of rootedness, in the short-to-medium term. By the same token, white-based commercial and industrial concerns with a large base of white shareholders can only absorb a certain number of blacks with expertise before their number peaks. I have argued that there are some advantages to this situation.

"It should not be expected that the levelling-off of black participation, and the subsequent limitation in black influence in such institutions, should lead to their destruction. On the contrary, the service they provide remains essential to the survival of the entire country. The perceived limitation in total black control results in the maintenance of essential productive capability and some measure of predictable stability. By the time a critical mass of blacks is in place, there will be an institutional tradition of company practices into which new members are socialised. This situation may not be desirable from the perspective of a short-term radical project. But such an understanding may be crucial for a long-range perspective.

"This long-term transitional process may have some particular benefits for a white society that has lost political power. It retains for them a certain measure of cultural familiarity, which assures them some basis for working levels of self-confidence. But to the extent that this domain of familiarity may consolidate itself into an autonomy of expectations located outside of the challenges of the new order, it may run aground and self-destruct in decay. To prevent such an outcome, it will have to ensure a large measure of buy-in by a critical mass of participant black members."[11]

All this suggests that traditionally black localities around the country will become new zones of economic growth and evolve complex economies built around meeting the needs of embedded black communities. The success of this historic trend will largely depend on an extensive distribution of inventive capacity in the scientific and entrepreneurial fields throughout the entire population, freeing us from the current dependence on limited white expertise.

While this development may emerge on its own, it will require a great deal of stimulation and steering in the form of complex public policy interventions. This may involve developing an active capacity to develop thirty-to-fifty-year planning scenarios, involving, at its centre, high-quality social planning which stresses the creation of functional and productive living environments throughout the country. From such a perspective, a great deal of current policy perspectives take on a fresh significance: urban and rural planning; a high-quality schooling system; life-long learning; adult basic education and training; strong provincial and consolidated local governments. The aim would be to maintain reasonable levels of service to privileged communities, while considerably improving service provision in traditionally black localities.

What is the connection between the critique of "whiteness" and what our response to it has been; the hegemonic growth of a Black Consciousness (not in the sense of the philosophy or movement associated with Steve Biko, although it may not exclude it, but rather, in the more fundamental sense of the inevitability of a particular kind of social process); and the project of development so essential to our finding the future?

It will be obvious that the flow of social influence is not going in one direction from the black to the white community. There is a two-way process setting itself up as a critical stabilising factor, as we negotiate change. Because the process will not always be smooth, it will require a great deal of negotiated positions. On balance, though, white South Africa will be called upon to make greater adjustments to black needs than the other way round. This is an essential condition for a shift in white identity in which "whiteness" can undergo an experiential transformation by absorbing a new cultural experience as an essential condition for achieving a new sense of cultural rootedness. That is why every white South African should be proud to speak, read and write at least one African language, and should be ashamed if they are not able to.

This matter of rootedness is important. For example, from a black perspective, whatever the economic merits of the case, it is difficult not to see the transfer of capital to big Western stock exchanges as "whiteness" delinking itself from the mire of its South African history, to explore opportunities of disengagement, where the home base is transformed into a satellite market revolving around powerful Western economies, to become a market to be exploited rather than a home to be served.

This kind of "flight of white capital" may represent white abandonment of responsibility towards the only history that can promise salvation to "whiteness". Whiteness has a responsibility to demonstrate its bona fides in this regard. Where is the primary locus of responsibility for white capital, built over centuries with black labour and unjust laws? Failure to come to terms with the morality of this question ensures the continuation of the culture of insensitivity and debilitating guilt.

In the past, "whiteness" proclaimed its civilising mission in Africa. In reality, any advantages for black people, where they occurred, were an unintended result rather than an intended objective. A historic opportunity has arisen now for white South Africa to participate in a humanistic revival of our country through a readiness to participate in the process of redress and reconciliation. This is on the understanding that the "heart of whiteness" will be hard put to reclaim its humanity without the restoration of dignity to the black body.

We are all familiar with the global sanctity of the white body. Wherever the white body is violated in the world, severe retribution follows somehow for the perpetrators, if they are non-white, regardless of the social status of the white body. The white body is inviolable, and that inviolability is in direct proportion to the global vulnerability of the black body. This leads me to think that if South African whiteness is a beneficiary of the protectiveness assured by international whiteness, it has an opportunity to write a new chapter in world history. It will have to come out from under the umbrella and repudiate it. Putting itself at risk, it will have to declare that it is home now, sharing in the vulnerability of other compatriot bodies. South African whiteness will declare that its dignity is inseparable from the dignity of black bodies.

The collapse of "white leadership" that would spearhead this process has been lamented. On second thought, perhaps this situation represents a singular opportunity. The collapse of "white leadership" ought to lead to the collapse of the notion of "black leadership". Where there is no "white leadership" to contest with "black leadership", where these descriptions of leadership were a function of an outmoded politics of a racist state, we are left only with leaders to lead this country. There can be no more compelling argument than this, to urge for care and caution in addressing the issue of racism in the southern tip of the African continent. The historic disintegration of "white leadership" imposes immense responsibilities on how we frame notions of leadership in the resultant political space we are now inheriting.

This way, the South African state is placed in a unique position to declare its obligations to all citizens. It should jealously and vigorously protect all bodies within its borders and beyond.

When I began to write this talk, I had no idea where it would take me. Faced with a daunting randomness, I settled on the themes of race, consciousness and social process around which to explore any possible ways into the future. I am humbled by the knowledge that there can never be one, single definitive way. There are many other possible paths.

Muzi Kuzwayo, in the conclusion to his fine book, tells the story of how, a year before the 1999 elections, a "white guy" who discovered that Muzi was in advertising, came to him with a bizarre proposal. He sought advice on how to market a coffin-manufacturing company, which would flourish from the violence being forecasted at the time, and from all the HIV/AIDS deaths. "I refused to help him," writes Muzi, "because I have faith in this country and its people. And every day my faith is reaffirmed by the millions who get on buses, trains and taxis to go to work.

"Lately, increasing crime, disease and interest rates are causing justified desperation. But I still have faith. And faith doesn't have to be justified. My future depends on South Africans spending their hard-earned money on bread, books, alcohol, savings or investment accounts, or anything else that keeps our economy going.

"If you are in marketing, advertising or any other industry, you must have faith. Irrational as it may be. Sometimes it will waver and when that happens remember those people who stockpiled tons of food, water and petrol before our first democratic election. They were all wrong."[12]

It is my act of faith in the act of writing that has got me where I am now with only a few ideas. And I thank you.

Notes

1 Millard Arnold (ed.). 1979. *Steve Biko: Black Consciousness in South Africa*. New York: Vintage Books, p. 344.
2 Arnold, *Steve Biko*, p. 355.
3 Arnold, *Steve Biko*, pp. 345–46.
4 Arnold, *Steve Biko*, p. 203.
5 Arnold, *Steve Biko*, p. 343.
6 Arnold, *Steve Biko*, p. 203.
7 Steve Biko. 2004 [1978]. *I Write What I Like*. Johannesburg: Picador Africa, p. 40.
8 Aelred Stubbs. 2004 [1978]. "Martyr of Hope: A Personal Memoir". In Biko, *I Write What I Like*, pp. 205–06.
9 Muzi Kuzwayo. 2000. *Marketing through Mud and Dust*. Cape Town: Ink Inc., p. 89.
10 Kuzwayo, *Marketing through Mud and Dust*, p. 57.
11 Njabulo Ndebele. 11 May 2000. "Finding Shared Memories". Paper delivered at the Inaugural Conference of the Institute for Justice and Reconciliation. Cape Town.
12 Kuzwayo, *Marketing through Mud and Dust*.

2

Biko's Children

Speaker: Prof. Zakes Mda
Date: 12 September 2001

"In Sesotho there is a saying: '*motjheka sediba ha a se nwe*' ('he who digs a well does not drink from it'). Only those who come after him will quench their thirst from its cool water. When the forebears formulated this adage, they had Steve Bantu Biko in mind, even as he sat in the world of pre-creation waiting to be created."

– *Zakes Mda*

Biko's Children

In Sesotho there is a saying: "*motjheka sediba ha a se nwe*" ("he who digs a well does not drink from it"). Only those who come after him will quench their thirst from its cool water. When the forebears formulated this adage, they had Steve Bantu Biko in mind, even as he sat in the world of pre-creation waiting to be created. When he finally came he became a digger of wells from which he never drank, since his life was cut short. As a drinker from the wells that he dug, I am honoured and humbled by the Steve Biko Foundation's invitation to deliver the second Steve Biko Memorial Lecture.

Recently I was invited to an inspiring event in the heart of Soweto that left me proud to be a South African – the Youth Empowerment and Networking Imbizo. The young woman who organised the event, a powerful performance poet called Lebo Mashile, told me that the objective of the *imbizo* was to inspire young people through art, and to motivate them to greater heights of creativity through the successes of peer role-models, with the view of creating a positive and productive youth community.

I had been for some time on the trail of dub poets who were signalling a new age of activism in their performances. The invitation promised performances by Tumi, Zee, Sammy, Lebo, Kano, Palesa, Makgabe, Miriam, Siphiwe, Mpho, Masello, Roots 200 and Delia – young men and women without surnames, who have been plying their consciousness-raising poetry in the various underground venues of Gauteng.

What was remarkable about this gathering was that it had not been decreed from above, perhaps by some youth commission, some government agency or even some non-governmental organisation that needed to justify its existence to some donor. At their own volition and expense, young people came together to create community dialogue on issues that concerned them most. And this, I was told, happened quite often. The whole movement is not institutional. It is a cultural and political reawakening of those who had been consigned to the ditches of a lost generation, who are now pulling themselves out, quite mercilessly, by the scruff of their necks.

The performances of the poets were interspersed with presentations from Black Rage, Loxion Kultcha and Blk Sonshine, initiatives by young people who had taken a creative concept and managed to implement it and make it financially viable in such fields as internet publishing, fashion design, production and music.

The presentations were followed by a workshop that explored what the participants referred to as "Universal Oppression". In the words of Lebo Mashile: "Most black people have the perception that oppression is something that is imposed from the 'top' down. Oppression begins with the self-perception that one is unworthy, unlovable, stupid, ignorant, good-for-nothing. One cannot impose on another that which they know to be untrue about themselves. Once a false self-image is ingrained in the individual psyche, oppression works more like a ripple in a pool. It is the feeling of powerlessness that inspires us to oppress others. When I feel as though I have been robbed of power, society has conditioned me to react by robbing others of their power, usually those that I deem less powerful than me. Thus the victim and oppressor are usually one and the same, but play different roles in different contexts."[1]

This process of self-examination and self-criticism is achieved through drama because, according to the facilitator, drama and creativity are effective outlets for the exploration of issues in a space where people feel safe enough to expose their vulnerability. Lebo Mashile says the use of drama and the creative arts has been essential to all struggles all over the planet, including our own struggle here in South Africa. It will continue to be essential in the new struggle against the enemy of self.

At this youth *imbizo*, I could hear echoes of the voices of the youth of the early 1970s, when Steve Biko and other leaders of the time espoused the philosophy of political and economic liberation that would emanate from the psychological liberation of the oppressed black masses. Indeed, I could see the young Matsemela Manaka of the 1970s in a poet from a Diepkloof-based outfit called C4 Tupperware from Mars (don't be put off by these names, they belie profound content). The movement may be reminiscent of the activism of the 1970s, but the poetry is fresh and new. Its form and content are of this age. It is mostly rhyming dub-influenced poetry that addresses the youths' disillusionment with post-liberation politics and politicians who, they feel, have betrayed them. But most importantly, the resounding message is that of self-assertion, self-development and psychological liberation through positive cultural action.

We remember that one of the greatest contributions of Steve Biko's Black Consciousness Movement was that of positioning culture at the centre of the liberation struggle, more than any other political movement had done before.

An early attempt to harness cultural action to the liberation struggle began and ended in the 1940s when prominent members of the African National Congress (ANC) Youth League mooted plans for the establishment of an African Academy. Through the African academy, African artists in all spheres of the arts would unite and interpret the spirit of Africa. The academy would also help African scholars break the dominance of white academics in African studies. The Programme of Action, a statement of policy authored by AP Mda, president of the ANC Youth League, and adopted at the ANC annual conference on 17 December 1949, stated that the theatre of struggle against white domination and for the attainment of political independence would not be confined to the political arena. The revolution would also be staged in the arenas of economics, education and culture. The document stressed the necessity of uniting the cultural with the educational and national struggle. And, of course, the establishment of a national academy of arts and sciences stood out as one of the key objectives.

With the advent of Black Consciousness, a protest culture that pervaded black South African life was converted into a resistance culture. This was reflected clearly in the practice of theatre – in its production and enjoyment. Whereas the predominant mode of political theatre before this era was a theatre of protest, the Black Consciousness movement gave birth to a theatre of resistance. I have written elsewhere that protest theatre made a statement of disapproval, but did not go beyond that. It addressed itself to the oppressor, with the view of appealing to his conscience. It was therefore a theatre of complaint, of weeping and of self-pity. It did not offer any solution beyond the depiction of the inhumanity of the system on passive victims. Its most famous practitioner was Athol Fugard with his plays that depicted various aspects of segregation and racial discrimination in South Africa. When Gibson Kente finally turned his hand to a theatre that had some political content, his work was also of the protest-theatre mode.

Black Consciousness was a philosophy of resistance rather than of protest. With it came a new generation of theatre practitioners, the Matsemela Manakas and the Maishe Maponyas, who created work that went beyond protest. This new theatre of resistance no longer placed the onus on the oppressed to prove their humanity. It no longer attempted to appeal to the conscience of the oppressor. It addressed itself directly to the oppressed, with the view of mobilising the oppressed to fight against oppression. Not only did this new militant theatre propagate messages of liberation, it agitated for action on the part of the oppressed to change their own situation. It was the theatre that was seen on professional stages. But it was also the theatre of street corners, of funerals, of weddings and of political rallies. Depending on the proficiency of its creators, it was a theatre of an artistry that lived beyond the occasion, but also it was a theatre of litanies and slogans.[2]

We also remember that Steve Biko and his colleagues did not only take our culture from a protest mode to that of challenge and resistance, they were hands-on activists who established practical community-development projects. These men and women went beyond moaning and whinging about the plight of the black people; they made their hands dirty with the soil of the land, building health-delivery centres and running them, and facilitating the establishment of communal gardens in marginalised communities. In this way, they aimed to inculcate values of self-reliance and self-development in addition to self-esteem, self-respect and self-confidence.

In my view, the young men and women without surnames are the true heirs of Biko, even more than factious political formations that profess to be the guardians of his legacy. Not only have these young people taken practical steps to inject consciousness into their lives through their art, to use culture to create a critical awareness of their situation and to mobilise themselves to action, but questions of self-esteem, self-reliance and self-development form the foundation of their philosophy. They have come to a conclusion that culture is the central tool for domination and must therefore be resisted by an alternative culture. Using the arts as a tool of analysing their society, they are rewriting the script of their lives in a manner that defies their imposed identity of a lost generation.

The various excluded South African groups can rewrite the script of their communities too if they embrace the ethos of self-development and self-reliance. Self-development is the kind of development that has not been imposed from above by so-called experts. It emanates from the community itself after the community has been equipped with the tools of critically analysing their society, engaging in a dialogue about their needs, and then adopting resolutions on what route to take to solve their problems. Only after this process is technical expertise from outside necessary. The reliance on the community's own mental and material resources – self-reliance, that is – engenders a sense of ownership of the development in question. This does not in any way imply the rejection of external resources, but these generally are used to supplement, enhance and enrich local resources. It does mean, however, the rejection of those external resources that are offered at the cost of the community's loss of self-respect and that impinge on the community's autonomy of choice of action. Self-reliance, of course, can only be achieved if the community has a critical awareness of its own creative assets. In many instances, cultural action has been effective in realising this awareness.

It is clear, therefore, that self-development and self-reliance are products of popular participation. South Africa is yet to learn that there can be no transformation without popular participation. Hence, we do not see any organised efforts to increase the people's control over their own institutions and resources. Popular participation in the transformation of South Africa has been rendered irrelevant by a government bent on centralising power at all levels. Even at the very village level, people are represented in local government structures by officials who have been deployed from outside those communities, in many instances as a reward for services rendered to the party. Local communities are regarded as spoils that must be shared at the table of expediency. I have visited many rural communities in the Free State and the Eastern Cape, and I have seen party officials at some district headquarters making decisions on behalf of villages they know nothing about. From a position of ignorance, *apparatchiks* are supposed to drive community development.

No wonder many of our developmental efforts have failed. We operate under the false notion that the meaning of development is confined to economic growth and technological advancement. We forget that the quality of life of the people will only improve when individual members of the community have achieved greater control of their institutions, and therefore of their social, economic and political destiny.

There is no doubt that our government has made great strides in the war against poverty in this country, especially in the areas of housing and provision of clean water, electricity and phones. Even in the much-maligned education arena the South African child is much better off than he or she ever was before. And there has been a great improvement in the delivery of primary health care, while tertiary health services are floundering. Another great stride that I see is in the development of human resources. We are enjoying an unprecedented period of freedom, and a human rights culture is beginning to crystallise – even though ugly intolerance does occasionally rear its head. Amazing things have happened in this country in a very short space of time.

Yet still, children are dying of malnutrition in the Eastern Cape, a region with the highest mortality rate for women and children in the whole of South Africa. Dire poverty covers the beautiful landscape that is inhabited by walking ghosts with sunken eyes. These are the excluded people of South Africa, and they are a clear indication that the government's strategy for rural development, if there is one, has failed. And its failure lies at the door of the politics of deployment and redeployment, where government officials and elected representatives are not accountable to the people but rather to party bosses.

One senses strong disillusionment with politicians among young South Africans, only seven years after the euphoria of 1994. And here I am not talking of the white youth who believe affirmative action has rendered their future meaningless in this country. I am talking of young black South Africans in the rural areas and marginalised urban ghettos, who see, rightly or wrongly, only bleakness in their future and blame politicians for betraying them. You hear it in their songs and in their poetry – works of art that are irreverent and have the potency of crushing political egos.

This is a good sign. It augurs well for the future of South Africa because post-colonial Africa (or neo-colonial Africa, if you like) has not been known for its vigilance against the excesses of its political leaders. Soon after independence, the youth were incorporated into the organs of a monolith whose function was to advance the cult of the personality of the political leader. He became the Chosen One, the Anointed One, and even the Saviour. Megalomania began to gel, and political leaders became infallible. This was accompanied by the complicity of African intellectuals in the deification of these nationalist leaders. The fate of the African peoples was sealed in the hands of corrupt buffoons who brooked no opposition. Even trade unions became mere labour desks of the ruling parties.

Thus, Africa was burdened with the Mobutu Sese Sekos and the Kamuzu Bandas, who ganged into an old boys' club that used the Organisation of African Unity (OAU) to safeguard their position through its non-interference clause. Today we see the results of that cult of the personality and the deification of political leaders in the person of Robert Mugabe of Zimbabwe. We also see the old boys' club mentality in the manner his brother-leaders from the SADC countries have grouped around him and played down his excesses, not only against white farmers, but against black Zimbabweans, for it is black Zimbabweans who have been the greatest casualties of his insanities.

Perhaps I should nail my colours to the mast as far as Zimbabwe is concerned, especially because there is a tendency in this country for black people to be reluctant to criticise Mugabe because that would place them on the same side as Tony Leon.

As a writer I have a close affinity to Zimbabwean writers, the Chenjerai Hoves and Yvonne Veras, whose work has greatly influenced mine. I have seen writers and other artists contributing in the liberation struggle by rallying people around the cause. I have seen their work celebrating a new Zimbabwe and a great future that everyone thought awaited Zimbabweans. I have seen the cult of the personality emerging around Mugabe, and I myself contributed to its creation, for, as a staunch pan-Africanist, Mugabe was my hero. I have seen the complicity of the trade union movement in that country. It was only much later that the Zimbabwean trade union movement woke up to the excesses of the ruling elite and assumed an independent voice. I have seen the usual complicity of the intellectuals. I remember Eddison Zvogbo, a senior cabinet minister in the Mugabe government and a poet of sorts, becoming a doyen of the denizens of the university staff club in Harare, where intellectuals would ply him with whisky while he plied them with socialist rhetoric. At the same time, he was accumulating hotels and farms for himself.

A culture of unbridled accumulation established itself in that country soon after independence in 1980. It spread and seeped deep into the walls of the halls of power in proportion to the increasing volume of socialist rhetoric emanating from every aperture of the ruling elite. It is only partly true that Mugabe was unable to address the land question because he was hamstrung by "sunset clauses" in the 1979 Lancaster House Agreement that set the stage for Zimbabwean independence. During the twenty years of the sunset clauses, Mugabe was able to dish out farms to his cronies and colleagues in an elaborate patronage system.

It is a fact that the white farmers in Zimbabwe have always obstructed land reform. But Mugabe's government had the option to exercise its power to introduce and enforce reforms through legal and constitutional means. If his had been a government worth its salt at all, it would have effectively dealt with that little problem. Mugabe failed his people. He failed to redress the inequities of colonialism in the twenty-one years he has been in power. Then he decides to render his country ungovernable to save his skin, sacrificing his country and its economy for short-term gains. A self-destructive ruse for the retention of power! In the meantime, the people of Soweto have their electrical power cut off when they default on payment while Eskom continues to feed endless supplies of current to a defaulting Zimbabwean government. The poor people of South Africa find themselves subsidising the excesses of a dictator.

The very intellectuals who helped create Mugabe's cult of the personality are at the receiving end of those excesses. Writers who used to sing the songs of that revolution are now under constant surveillance from the Central Intelligence Organisation. Those who speak out are given a thorough hiding by the members of the youth organisation of the ruling party and by the so-called war veterans. No one is ever charged for such gross violations of human rights.

In South Africa, we are beginning to see the emergence of a similar culture of unbridled accumulation. Unlike the ruling elites of Zimbabwe who garnished their accumulation with socialist rhetoric, our ruling elites have discarded any pretensions to socialism. Instead, they have adopted a new slogan: "Accumulation cannot be democratised". We hear this repeated at their cocktail parties and at every self-congratulatory gathering. We see a culture of conspicuous consumption and instant gratification giving birth to wholesale corruption. We also see the arrogance of power gradually turning into racial arrogance: black people are not supposed to criticise black people, otherwise they are playing into the hands of racist whites who do not think blacks can run this country without taking it down the sewers.

This antipathy to public debate about our strengths and weaknesses is a symptom of our lack of self-confidence and self-esteem. We seem to forget that we are in power now. We should get on with running the country unapologetically instead of whining and whinging about how much of an unfair deal we are getting from our racist compatriots, from foreign investors and from the media. Yes, most of our media have replaced scepticism with cynicism when it comes to the government. But from where I am standing, this is a lesser evil than the media that I saw eulogising the nationalist leaders in newly independent Africa, glossing over their weaknesses, and reflecting on their looting of the coffers of the state as due rewards for sacrifices made in the fight for liberation. This continued unabated until we reached a stage where news became news only if it had something to do with the president's speech or with a cabinet minister opening a new conference centre.

The constant looking over our collective shoulder in fear of racist judgement of our conduct and performance has stifled the self-examination and self-criticism that is essential for community development. But fortunately, as I have indicated, the young people of South Africa do not subscribe to this antipathy. A young playwright, Xoli Norman, has written a powerful play titled *Hallelujah!* It has been enjoying a season of full houses at the Market Theatre. The play addresses, among other issues, black people's self-hatred, which manifests itself in their interactions among themselves and with black people from other parts of the continent. After one performance a black journalist commented: "This playwright is exposing us to the whites. What he is saying in his play is true, but must not be said in a public forum because it reinforces racist notions about blacks". It was therefore gratifying to hear a young member of the audience respond, "But Steve Biko said we need self-criticism in order to liberate ourselves. Black Consciousness was conceived with the view of getting rid of the very self-hatred that Norman writes about".

The strength of our political development in South Africa lies in the fact that we did not develop a cult of the personality. As much as some of our honoured freedom fighters would have liked to be reincarnated into parliamentary political life as demigods, we refused to let that happen – although we almost canonised a living Nelson Mandela into sainthood. It is to his credit that he publicly revolted against deification. It is also to the credit of his generation of freedom fighters who continue to lead humble lives devoid of the vulgarities demonstrated by our new national elites. But the age of humility is passing. We have seen Govan Mbeki depart. Walter and Albertina Sisulu and a very few others remain the bearers of this humility. In no time, we shall be confronted head-on by the age of arrogance. The signs are there already.

Some of the signs lie in the politics of deployment and redeployment that I mentioned earlier. My concern is in its effect at the very grassroots level in the rural areas of South Africa. Its effect at national level has been discussed extensively. I myself have written about a number of highly qualified black South Africans who have opted to leave the country because the jobs for which they were qualified were given to political cronies and family members of the ruling elites who had zero qualifications in those fields, but who received huge salaries while their jobs were done by highly paid consultants.³ That trend continues today. Recently, a young, highly talented black woman went back to exile in Canada after discovering that affirmative action in practice does not really affirm black South Africans but rather black ruling-party faithfuls. Another talented young black South African, Majakathata Mokoena, wrote that the economy of South Africa had the potential to be the strongest in the southern hemisphere, and could support jobs for many people in southern Africa. But it is lagging behind because of what he calls crony capitalism. He writes:

> Crony capitalism is based on who one knows in the political body rather than on those who are well disposed to entrepreneurship and new business formation. That includes people who have gone to school to study business and other technocratic qualifications so that they can contribute positively to the growth of the country's economy. Now all these people's efforts are wasted while economically inept people are put in positions they barely understand. That is why there are so many failures in the new SA, despite the country's potential.⁴

With weak opposition parties that are only able to proffer right-wing and reactionary solutions to the problems of this country, and that are unable to deal with the government's arrogance of power, the trade union movement is a source of hope for many South Africans. The feeling is that even though it is part of the ruling alliance, it has not lost its independent voice. But in my book, the trade union leaders in this country have not acquitted themselves with any measure of brilliance or even integrity. They have used the workers as stepping-stones for the accumulation of untold personal wealth. They have ridden on the backs of the workers to the corridors of political power. After they had attained it, they soon forgot about their constituents. It was therefore difficult to take Zwelinzima Vavi seriously when he declared on SABC television on 30 August 2001, "We have no ambition of becoming full-time politicians. We have no wish of going to parliament."[5]

But facts speak a different language. The government has been able to silence trade union opposition by offering union leaders fat posts in the national and provincial governments, and by deploying them to the corporate world, where they implement the very policies they had been screaming against. Of course, one day the posts will be exhausted, and we shall see a trade union movement leadership that genuinely looks after the interests of the workers without using them for a cheap ride to self-aggrandisement. Perhaps Vavi's declaration is a signal that that is beginning to happen.

The effects of the politics of deployment and redeployment on rural development have not been discussed. I have indicated that the failure of the government's rural-development strategies lies in the lack of participation of the communities concerned in mapping out their own development. Plans are conceived by experts from outside the community, without the community's involvement in identifying their problems and in working out solutions from their own perspective. The rural poor are never involved in the design, implementation and evaluation of the projects. The notion of development in this country is that the centre must "deliver" development to the periphery, which must remain a passive beneficiary of whatever services and materials are delivered. The people's role as makers of history is negated. This concept of "delivery" has created and reinforced a dependency mentality on the people. Hence, people now expect their lot to improve without any agency on their part. They have been socialised into that kind of thinking.

Empirical studies have shown that participation of local communities and their organisations has improved performance in many urban and rural poverty-alleviation projects.[6] But South Africa cannot achieve any level of participation with its penchant for the centralisation of power, where everyone is subject to what the centre decrees.

In my experience in the rural areas, local government representatives who have been imposed on the villages, and therefore are not accountable to the villagers but to party bosses, have stifled those development initiatives by members of the community in which the local government representatives did not have a stake. In some villages, a project must first be approved by party structures before it can be put before government and non-governmental structures. There is no longer a distinction in the village between a party and a government structure.

Our movement away from a people-centred government to a government by deployment breeds the arrogance of power. The arrogance of power goes hand-in-glove with corruption. But rural development is not only thwarted by corruption at the local level. The biggest constraint to development is corruption at the centre where funding from our taxes and from the donor community is controlled. Ineptitude and inefficiency also play their part.

We have heard of the six executive directors of the National Development Agency who pay themselves R450 000 each while the agency fails to disburse funds to struggling poverty-alleviation projects.

An example of a community-development project that has suffered because of the unsavoury practices of the national elites is the Lower Telle Beekeepers Collective. This was established two years ago by members of a village community in the Herschel district of the Eastern Cape after going through a process of critically examining their situation. Village men used to work on the mines, and women used to trek to the Free State farms for seasonal employment at harvest time. But retrenchments, both in the mines and at the farms, have taken their toll. The vast majority of the people of Lower Telle are unemployed. The village is located on a rocky mountain and only small strips on the banks of the river are suitable for agriculture. But the mountains are rich in aloes whose flowers produce nectar and pollen that is natural food for bees. So the people decided to form a beekeeping collective – a development project that would rely on their own mental and material resources, using raw material that exists in abundance in their community. But to achieve this they needed technical expertise and financial resources from outside the community. Their application for assistance, which included training in beekeeping and initial stock, was approved by a development foundation of a big parastatal. But before any assistance could be disbursed, the ugly head of corruption reared its head. All funding was suspended by the foundation while it undertook a forensic audit because the foundation's chief executive had either mismanaged or embezzled some funds. Once again, the rural poor had to swim in the quagmire of their poverty while the national elites stuffed themselves like pigs from their ill-gotten spoils. It took almost two years for the problem to be resolved, and for forty families in some remote mountain village to realise their dream of establishing their own business from which they could feed their families and send their children to school.

Because I want to make a certain proposal to the audience that is gathered here tonight, I must add that I have been intimately involved with the Lower Telle Beekeepers Collective from its inception. I was a catalyst or a facilitator in the community's process of critically analysing their problems and in working out solutions from their perspective. I even took a beekeeping course in order to participate meaningfully in their activities.

I began this talk with Biko's children – the young men and women from marginalised communities who are using the arts to understand the nature of oppression (which includes the sources of poverty) and to liberate themselves from it. These youths are striving to put content back into their art and their lives. It is the duty of our society to support them in the generation of alternative values. It was, therefore, wonderful to learn that in June the Steve Biko Foundation launched the Expression of Identity Programme, a youth arts programme that encourages the adoption and reinforcement of the values I am discussing here. The Foundation has worked with some of the poets I have mentioned, and a group of them is taking a pilgrimage to King William's Town for a youth heritage festival from 22 to 24 September.

I end this lecture by throwing down a challenge to our black professionals in the public and private sectors in all the cities of South Africa to continue the legacy of Steve Biko. We have seen how Steve Biko and his colleagues did not dwell on high-flown philosophies that had no practical relevance to the lives of the people. They took practical steps to transform society at the very grassroots level. They conceived and established community-development projects. We can continue the Biko legacy by doing the same. Black professionals can adopt a village and act as catalysts or facilitators for its development, in the same manner that I did with my ancestral village of Lower Telle.

All black people in South Africa have a link with some village. Even those who are fourth-generation city dwellers, as you will find in townships like Soweto, have a village where their great-grandfather's umbilical cord was buried. Go back to that village and facilitate community dialogue on the issues that concern the villagers. Help the villagers to establish collectives and co-operative societies that use appropriate technology to exploit the raw materials that are found in any community. And this, of course, includes the raw talent of the youth in the arts and other facets of life. Be a catalyst for a people-centred development. This has no financial implications for you, except perhaps the cost of going there. And it will only take one weekend a month to achieve something that will, for example, save thousands of babies from dying of malnutrition. After a few months, when the project can stand on its own, you won't be needed anymore, except perhaps as an honorary adviser. After training in basic business methods, the villagers can run their projects themselves. There are many non-governmental organisations that specialise in this kind of training.

Rural development is the key to many of our problems, including that of the children who die of malnutrition in the Eastern Cape. But this would also contribute towards the reduction of crime and grime in the cities.

My challenge is further directed to Black Economic Empowerment (BEE) companies to establish foundations of the ilk of the Eskom Development Foundation to fund the individual projects of this Adopt-a-Village Campaign. It is very unfortunate that BEE companies are perceived to be reluctant to plough back into the community. The young people of the *imbizo* expressed the same sentiments. Lebo Mashile said about their attempts to fight poverty: "There is nothing noble about poverty. But young people with ideas do not get any assistance from black empowerment corporations. The people in these corporations have climbed up and reached the top. Now they kick the ladder."[7]

We know that the main reason BEE corporations have fallen short of their responsibility to the black community is that in many of these corporations the leadership is that of a new South Africa, while the content remains that of the old South Africa. This is clearly illustrated by a big corporation with a strong BEE component that refused to sponsor a television programme meant to cultivate a culture of reading, particularly in black communities, in support of Kader Asmal's Masifunde Sonke Campaign, but which is now sponsoring an idiotic programme called *Big Brother* on M-Net. Today there is no book-review programme on South African television and *Big Brother* thrives, thanks partly to black empowerment.

Of course, the corporation will say it is in business and is more interested in the mileage that it will get from *Big Brother*. But there is such a thing as social responsibility.

My emphasis is on BEE companies to fund the Adopt-a-Village Campaign because they have a special duty to do so, but in reality it is the task of the South African corporate world as a whole to fund such endeavours and to make Biko's children realise their potential.

An investment in Biko's children is an investment in the future of

South Africa, for they will not desert this country. It is their heritage. The Biko Foundation has launched development programmes in Ginsberg Township, much along the lines of the Adopt-a-Village Campaign that I am proposing here. The question I want to ask the Foundation is this: would they be willing to spearhead the Adopt-a-Village Campaign nationwide?

Notes

1 Lebo Mashile. 2001. Presentation delivered at the Youth Empowerment and Networking Imbizo. Soweto.
2 For a more detailed discussion on the various modes of South African theatre see: Zakes Mda. 1996. "Introduction: An Overview of Theatre in South Africa". In Zakes Mda (ed.). *Four Plays*. Johannesburg: Vivlia Publishers. See also Zakes Mda. "Theater and Reconciliation in South Africa". In *Theater* 25, 3: 38.
3 Zakes Mda. 14–20 February 1997. "Why we are Losing our Top Black Pros". *Mail & Guardian*.
4 Majakathata Mokoena. 29 July 2001. "The Nation is Greater than those with Political Power". *City Press*.
5 Zwelenzima Vavi. 30 August 2001. Statement made on a South African Broadcasting Corporation (SABC) show. Johannesburg.
6 See, for instance, Matthias Stiefel and Marshall Wolfe. 1994. *A Voice for the Excluded: Popular Participation in Development – Utopia or Necessity?* London: Zed Books.
7 Mashile, Youth Empowerment and Networking Imbizo.

3

Fighting Apartheid with Words

Speaker: Prof. Chinua Achebe
Date: 12 September 2002

"A young man with a sharp intellect and a flair for organisation and leadership, Biko realised the need to raise the sagging morale of black people, to raise their consciousness and self-esteem; in his own words to 'overcome the psychological oppression of black people by whites'."

– *Chinua Achebe*

Fighting Apartheid with Words

In early 1961, a few months after Nigeria was granted independence by Britain, I set out on my first African journey beyond the familiar bounds of my West African home. I planned to visit two regions – East Africa and Southern Africa. In the first six weeks I had "done" Kenya, Uganda, Tanganyika and Zanzibar. It had been, by no means, plain sailing. The first touch-down, in Nairobi, was preceded by an astonishing immigration ritual in the air. The landing card distributed to passengers asked them to indicate their identity as (1) European; (2) Asiatic; (3) Arab; (4) Other. I realised then that I was heading into interesting times; and I was not disappointed, so to speak. I realise that to you, my experiences in East Africa would seem tame and not worth talking about. I mention this only because it was my first "racial" experience, and it still stands out in my memory for the jolt it gave me; I had so little experience of dealing with the cruder forms of racial abuse. But, as I ended my six weeks in East Africa and turned southwards, my problems had increased enormously. I dare say, however, that even those would not merit discussion here. But they were enough to make me call off my voyage of discovery and return home. I knew that some day, after Southern Africa's liberation from racial oppression, I would complete my journey. I must say, however, that in 1961 the prospect seemed very distant indeed.

But, miracle of miracles, it happened in 1994! I should have been in the first crowd arriving to verify the incredible story with their own eyes and, like the magi, taking it back to their places, these kingdoms. Unfortunately, my ability to get up and go had been severely curtailed three years earlier in a quotidian voyage within Nigeria, and so I am this late in coming. But sooner or later, here I am. And to make up for my slowness, I have brought my wife and children to make it a big family visit.

A visit that was forty years in the making might be expected to come with a memorable message. I have brought the simplest of words – THANK YOU. Thank you for the epic struggle you waged for South Africa, for all of us in Africa, and for all peoples oppressed and their oppressors everywhere in the world. I say thank you to Nelson Mandela and his colleagues who inspired and led that heroic struggle. I say Thank You to all the people of South Africa – men, women, even children who came out in support, too often with their lives.

I want to thank the Steve Biko Foundation who took the initiative to invite me at this particular time, the twenty-fith year of Biko's death, to deliver the third Steve Biko Memorial Lecture, and who made all the complicated and expensive arrangements for our visit. I consider it the highest of privileges.

It is a particular honour, and a rare privilege and pleasure to have the Chancellor of the University of Cape Town presiding at this special Convocation. The admirable Graça Machel has a name to conjure with in post-colonial Africa and beyond. Thank you, ma'am.

And to my friend and fellow writer, Njabulo Ndebele, I owe special gratitude for this opportunity to address a great university. I appreciate the honorary Doctor of Literature you have thrown into the bargain. I must tell you I love honorary doctorates and have never understood why anybody should still want to get a doctorate degree the hard way. This is infinitely better.

My gratitude to my introducer, Nuruddin Farah – a long-time friend and an admirable novelist – who has stepped forward more than once in the past to pay tribute to my work.

Twenty-five years ago the government of South Africa added to its bad record of racial oppression the brutal murder of a young black man, Steve Biko – a student activist with a burning passion for freedom and equality in his native land, a prophet impatient for change and fairness.

Steve Bantu Biko was born on 18 December 1946. He died on 12 September 1977, three months before his thirty-first birthday. He had come of age in that bleak period of discouragement and despair following the banning of the ANC and the locking up of its leadership for good, as it seemed. A young man with a sharp intellect and a flair for organisation and leadership, Biko realised the need to raise the sagging morale of black people, to raise their consciousness and self-esteem; in his own words to "overcome the psychological oppression of black people by whites".[1]

Biko's encounter with the South African police was inevitable; it finally came in 1973 when a banning order was clamped on him. Two years later, in 1975, he was arrested and imprisoned for four months without charge or trial. The following year, 1976, he was held for over three months. In 1977 he was held in March, then again in July, and finally he was arrested at a roadblock and imprisoned in Port Elizabeth. For twenty-four days he was held naked and manacled in his cell and was severely beaten. Post-mortem examination would show three severe wounds to his head "caused by the application of force to his head".[2] In a state of unconsciousness he was carried in the back of a truck to Pretoria, 1 200 kilometres away. An inquest would later find the police not guilty of wrong-doing.

My excuse for this short recital of a story you know much better than I, is to indicate with one or two examples how faithfully South African literature, particularly its fiction, has played the role of witness to this country's appalling history, and why it was able to do so.

The death of Steve Biko is almost straight out of Alex La Guma's novella, *A Walk in the Night,* first published in Nigeria in 1962, fifteen years before Biko's dreadful ordeal.

A Walk in the Night is a densely packed story of one hell of a night in District Six, a neighbourhood where, in the words of the narrator, "people are thrown together in the whirlpool world of poverty, petty crime and violence".[3]

La Guma does not give us political or any other commentary on District Six; he gives us instead a dizzying succession of unforgettable images. For example, he introduces us to perhaps the only gentle person in the entire story – a homeless, eccentric boy called Joe who is going up the street "trailing his tattered raincoat behind him like a sword-slashed, bullet-ripped banner just rescued from a battle".[4]

A few lines later, La Guma gives us what amounts to a companion image, of two policemen on the beat: "They strolled slowly and determinedly side by side ... cutting a path through the stream on the pavement, like destroyers at sea."[5]

The reader's mental walk through this harrowing night in District Six ends with the quite unbearable portrayal of the death of another young character, Willieboy, hunted down remorselessly for a crime he did not even commit, shot and gravely wounded by a trigger-happy policeman on patrol, Constable Raalt. Raalt's patrol-mate and driver is quietly unhappy at the shooting and suggests they call an ambulance – a suggestion Constable Raalt sneeringly overrules. They throw the wounded boy in the back of their van and drive away from a gathering crowd in an ugly mood. On their way to the police station Raalt orders the driver to stop at a roadside bar for him to buy cigarettes and have a little chat.

It seems to me quite apparent that a literature which draws its sustenance from the life lived around it and develops imaginative identification with that life has a good chance of achieving the quality and the authority of prophetic utterance. Alex La Guma knew District Six like the palm of his hand. He was born there and grew up there. He knew the poverty, the despair, the alcohol, the squalor, the pain. He knew apartheid South Africa, the police and their ways. He knew the country's obsession with skin colour and hair texture. He was political; he joined trade unions, organised a strike and was fired from his job. Add all this to his brilliance as a story-teller, and you have a seer and prophet of the South African racial malaise.

Biblical scholars tell us that the Old Testament prophets performed a dual function – to foretell and to forth tell; to predict the future and to speak out against the ills of the present. Alex La Guma exemplified and fulfilled this dual mandate in his life and work, as did so many of his contemporaries.

In 1962 when *A Walk in the Night* was published, apartheid was at the height of its vigour, virulence and arrogance.

Almost twenty years later, in 1981, Nadine Gordimer published *July's People*, a prophecy about the end of apartheid in a violent revolution. The interesting thing about this prophecy is that it did not come about, although it had seemed so inevitable. As we now know – to our great relief – South Africa performed the miracle of an orderly transition from fascism to democracy. What happened? Was there indeed a miracle, or was Nadine Gordimer's prophetic vision somehow flawed? I think it might be helpful to consider this question alongside another novel bearing a prophecy that also apparently failed. I refer, of course, to George Orwell's *Nineteen Eighty-four*, a dreadful story of a waxing totalitarian state which holds its citizens hostage through brainwashing, perversion of language and perpetual surveillance by a "Thought Police".[6] Such was the impact of Orwell's novel on the world that words and phrases, such as "Big Brother" and "1984" itself have gone straight out of its pages into political language and even everyday speech.

As a very young man, George Orwell had gone from Eton College to work in the Indian Police in Burma in the heyday of British imperialism. But he was quickly disillusioned by the imperial vocation. His subsequent experiences included fighting in the Spanish Civil War and living the life of a tramp in England and France. He was clearly a political animal looking for an acceptable position in the highly ideological 1930s – when capitalism, communism, fascism and socialism struggled for ascendancy.

What I am getting at is that people who write books whose vocabulary moves into common speech, or whose imagery grips the popular imagination, do not stumble accidentally into their status; they achieve it through the deep knowledge they have acquired, often painfully, about their society. With the power and authority of this status George Orwell became a prophet able to scare the world with the starkness and urgency of his vision and, perhaps, make us a little better behaved than we were inclined ordinarily to be. There was a deep sigh of relief in many places when the year 1984 finally came and the nightmare world of Orwell's imagination did not happen. The English novelist and critic Anthony Burgess celebrated the non-event with the publication in 1984 of a book he called *Ninety-nine Novels: the best in English since 1939* – as though to take our minds off the narrow escape we had just had.

Alex La Guma knew his South Africa thoroughly and left us indispensable images of the cruelty of apartheid at the height of its notoriety. Or take another writer: Nadine Gordimer's literary career began simultaneously with the birth of apartheid. From her close and attentive observation she gave us a scenario for its imminent fall convincing enough to give a healthy scare to her headstrong countrymen.

Although apartheid is gone, the legacy of Steve Biko will grow in this country and in Africa for the clarity of his political thought and for his physical and moral courage. One will inevitably hear criticisms and reservations concerning his strong language about white liberals, and for such actions as his alleged abandonment of a multiracial student organisation in order to found an all-black association. One will hear, I am sure, the handy phrase "reverse racism". But Biko insisted that what he saw was not a multiracial, but rather a pseudo-multiracial, organisation in which "the whites [were] doing all the talking and blacks [all] the listening".[7] He understood that hundreds of years of discrimination and dispossession of black people in South Africa had seriously damaged their self-esteem. For a young man in his twenties, brilliant and impatient for freedom, Steve Biko's rhetoric was neither extravagant nor out of place. His insistence that black people and their white liberal associates should take a hard, critical look at their relationship was appropriate, and really no different from Nadine Gordimer's X-ray examination of that same problematic relationship in *July's People* and indeed in practically all her work. And it is not even a peculiarly South African necessity. It was, for example, a major concern in the civil rights movement in America. I do recall watching a short dramatic sketch on an off-off-Broadway stage in New York in the late 1960s. The play opened with a group of black revolutionaries discussing their plan of action, with one white liberal in their midst. Their plan, it turned out, was to kidnap Mrs Kennedy, the president's wife, during a visit to New York. The white liberal was opposed to this project and argued very strongly against it. In the second and final scene the same people were in the same room, in the same posture, still discussing their plan. But something had changed. They were now discussing how to kidnap not Jacqueline Kennedy but Martin Luther King.

You might say that was a rather bizarre way to pose a perennial question: How much credence can a victim of racial oppression place on the disinterestedness of any member of the oppressor group who is, or claims to be, a liberal sympathiser while enjoying the benefits conferred automatically on him by his skin colour? Is it fair that the victim should be saddled with the additional burden of sorting out this ambiguity when all his energies should be channelled into his struggle?

I hope you will believe me when I say that I am not in the habit of going about knocking liberals; I really don't think that the awkwardness in their condition should be blamed on the likes of Steve Biko, but rather on those whose racial arrogance, greed and stupidity made skin colour such a red flag in the first place. In a decent, humane society, Steve Biko would have been cherished as a young man of great promise; even when in youthful conceit he could say that "it was a waste of time to try and change the mind of anybody over forty, as they have already made up their minds"[8], his countrymen over forty should have bestowed on him an indulgent smile rather than a barbaric execution.

The sum total of what I have been trying to say is congratulations to the good people of South Africa for bringing the long nightmare of apartheid to an end; to the brave warriors who took on the enemy on every theatre of that war; to the writers, in particular to the very first South African writer I ever met – Es'kia Mphahlele, the doyen of African literature; novelist, short story writer, autobiographer, critic, scholar, teacher. And then the group of gifted writers I met in exile in America in the 1970s – Willie Kgosietsile, Dennis Brutus, Bloke Modisane, Lewis Nkosi, Daniel and Mazisi Kunene and Bessie Head. I should mention here the poets Mafika Gwala, Mongane Serote, Sipho Sepamla, and Oswald Mtshali. The list goes on and on and I think I should invoke the Igbo wisdom which says that when you have 400 dignitaries to salute, you can either go on doggedly and call each man by his title, or you can wave your hand over the crowd and speak the formula: every man and his own and that magic phrase – "*onye na nke ya*" – absolves you from the obligation to remember and pronounce 400 salutations.

But it is particularly important to recognise the high hopes we have for a great literary harvest in the post-apartheid era. These hopes are encouraged by the work of a vibrant group of new writers. I hope your promise will be fulfilled in abundance. If you don't mind, I will leave a word of advice with you. If someone comes from afar and tells you admiringly that you are Africa's answer to Latin American magic realism, or something equally profound, you should smile and slip away as soon as you can. Your admirer has obviously never heard about Africa's oral tradition, nor about that incredible Igbo cultural event called *mbari* in which gods and people and beasts real or imaginary assemble on one grand concourse to celebrate the spirit of creativity; and finally, he has never heard of Amos Tutuola, a Yoruba Nigerian coppersmith who began publishing magic realism in 1954 without hearing about Latin America. You must learn to relish the adoring presence of the world at your doorstep but remember that if you buy every ware it peddles on the side, you will be broke.

I cannot end my salutes without giving the biggest one to Mrs Biko who made such a heart-breaking sacrifice to South Africa.

Earlier this year, I saw on American television an interview of Mr

Mandela on the *Oprah Winfrey Show*. Oprah was suitably deferential, but there was something she refused to accept. Mr Mandela was at pains to explain to her that the victory was not his alone but the work of a group and the whole country. He kept stressing the collegiate, the co-operative; she kept insisting on the self, the individual. It all seemed to me like a little war game between the Western and African psychologies, between "I think, therefore I am" and "A human is human because of other humans". South Africa's victory over apartheid will teach many powerful lessons to the world. Archbishop Desmond Tutu's Truth and Reconciliation Commission is one lesson. The fact that President Nelson Mandela stepped down for a successor after five years – in a continent of presidents-for-life – is another.

Because your success was so great, you have, and are entitled to have, the highest expectations of dividends. The leaders whom you have chosen to manage the assets of this beautiful land on your behalf, have the responsibility to address those high expectations. Along with your well-wishers in Africa and around the world, I wish you and President Mbeki and his government great success.

Notes

1 Steve Biko. Unknown source.
2 Aelred Stubbs. 1978. In Aelred Stubbs (ed.). Steve Biko. *I Write What I Like*. London: Bowerdean Press.
3 Alex la Guma. 1962. *A Walk in the Night*. Ibadan: Mbari Publications.
4 La Guma, *A Walk in the Night*.
5 La Guma, *A Walk in the Night*.
6 George Orwell. 2002 [1949]. *Nineteen Eighty-Four*. London: Penguin.
7 Steve Biko. 2004 [1978]. *I Write What I Like*. Johannesburg: Picador Africa, p. 21.
8 Steve Biko. Unknown source.

4

Recovering our Memory:
South Africa in the Black Imagination

Speaker: Ngugi wa Thiong'o
Date: 12 September 2003

"Steve Biko, whom we have come to honour, is among this great gallery of people whose work and devotion have impacted those beyond the native shores, and which make it possible for us even to talk about the possibilities of a new Africa out of the colonial ashes of latter-day empires."
– *Ngugi wa Thiong'o*

Recovering our Memory:
South Africa in the Black Imagination

When Vasco da Gama set foot in the Cape in 1498, it was part of the general period of what has come to be known as the European renaissance, the founding moment of capitalist modernity and Western bourgeois ascendancy in the world. It was also the beginning of the wanton destruction of many city civilisations along the coasts of Africa, East Africa in particular. In 1994, Nelson Mandela, as the first black president of the Republic of South Africa at a meeting of the OAU in Tunis, recalled the destruction of Carthage by the generals of an earlier empire and said: "Where South Africa appears on the agenda again, let it be because we want to discuss what its contribution shall be to the making of the new African Renaissance. Let it be because we want to discuss what materials it will supply for the rebuilding of the African city of Carthage".[1] In a way, South Africa has already supplied such material by way of men and women whose lives and actions and thoughts have made South Africa an integral part of the black self-imagination. Steve Biko, whom we have come to honour, is among this great gallery of people whose work and devotion have impacted those beyond the native shores, and which make it possible for us even to talk about the possibilities of a new Africa out of the colonial ashes of latter-day empires.

I therefore feel honoured, humbled in fact, to have been asked to give the fourth annual Steve Biko Memorial Lecture in memory of this illustrious son of the soil. He combines the cultural, the intellectual and the political in the same person. He exemplifies the public intellectual in its finest tradition. In one of his interviews reproduced in *I Write What I Like*, Biko describes a confrontation with his jailers in which he asserts his right to resistance for as long as he is able.

"If you guys want to do this your way," he tells his jailers, "you have got to handcuff me and bind my feet together, so that I can't respond. If you allow me to respond, I'm certainly going to respond. And I'm afraid you may have to kill me in the process even if it's not your intention."[2]

The words spoken in 1976 a few months before his brutal murder are evocative of others spoken earlier in 1964 by Mandela from the dock at the Rivonia trial where, in expressing his ideal of a democratic and free society, he reaffirms his commitment to live for and to achieve the ideal: "But if needs be, it is an ideal for which I am prepared to die."[3] One eventually went to prison for twenty-seven years; the other died in prison in a prophetic fulfilment of his words: "It is better to die for an idea that lives, than to live for an idea that dies."[4]

In both cases, their words and lives add to the rich intellectual legacy of African heroes and heroines of pan-African struggles, a legacy summed up in Robert Sobukwe's words: "It is meet that we tell the truth before we die."[5] One associates Sobukwe and Biko with Black Consciousness, Mandela with the Renaissance. But it is significant for me that the three lives, while inextricably linked to black and social imagination everywhere, are South African, and the concepts of consciousness and renaissance have found new life in South Africa today.

As a Kenyan, an African and a writer, South Africa holds a special place in my social experience and intellectual formation. It was as an educational presence that I first became aware of this country. I had just started primary schooling when it was announced that one of our teachers, moreover from my village, was leaving us. He was going to Fort Hare for more learning. The image of Fort Hare as a Mecca of learning was reinforced when later, yet another from the same region, this time a minister of religion, followed suit.

However, it was while I was a student in an independent African school that I first became aware of the South African story as also being my own story. The independent African-run schools in Kenya were started in the 1930s and their coming into being had been inspired by the Ethiopian movement in South, Central and East Africa. But it was the way our teacher taught the South African story, from the perspective of the black experience, that brought it home to us, and the names of Shaka, Moshoeshoe and Cetshwayo became part of our collective memory.

When the Mau Mau war for Kenya's independence started in 1952, the colonial administration reacted by closing these schools down or taking them over, and this time the story of South Africa became that of Vasco da Gama, Kruger, the Great Trek and, of course, General Smuts.

Fortunately, the other image of the South African story as my story never disappeared. In fact it was rekindled with greater intensity when later, in high school, a missionary-run school, I saw one of the only two African teachers in the school holding a copy of Peter Abrahams', *Tell Freedom*. It is difficult to quite describe the impact of the title on my imagination, encountering it, as I did, when Kenya was in the midst of the War of Independence. The title was to lead me to the works of Abrahams and to the great gallery of South African writers, some of whom I was later to interact with as fellow writers and friends.

I cannot forget the impact of Mphahlele on African writing in general and on Kenyans in particular. His Chemchemi Cultural Centre in Nairobi in the early years of our independence became truly a spring for young Kenyan talent. His struggles for the African image as that of an assertive sovereign subject, acting on his environment, resonated with me, growing up, as I did, in the shadow of the colonial white image of the African as an object without agency, always acted upon.

By exploring the issue of human inferiority, these writers, artists and musicians told the human dimension of what was being enacted in the open theatre of organised politics which had also produced heroes and heroines who became expressions of our own struggles. I cannot think of another country which has produced so many names from so many walks of life which have become part of the African experience, using the term African in its pregnant inclusiveness, as used in Thabo Mbeki's 1996 address to the constitutional assembly: "I am an African".[6]

Not surprisingly, South Africa is always on my mind. At the United Nations Children's Fund (UNICEF) conference on the situation of children in Southern Africa held in Harare in March 1988, I opened my talk on the role of intellectual workers with the assertion that the liberation of South Africa was the key to the social liberation of the continent.

Later, in April 1990, in an article celebrating the release of Nelson Mandela, I came back to the same theme, the place of South Africa in the black self-imagination, and claimed that South Africa was a mirror of the emergence of the modern world. I was not saying anything new. No less a figure than Adam Smith of *The Wealth of Nations* fame was to cite the discovery of America and that of a passage to the East Indies via the Cape of Good Hope, as two of the greatest and most important events recorded in human history, a claim repeated in the nineteenth century by Marx and Engels in *The Communist Manifesto,* where they argue that the consequences of the twin events gave to commerce, to navigation, to industry, an impulse never before known, and therefore, to the revolutionary element in the tottering feudal society, a rapid development.[7]

Adam Smith was to wonder about the benefits or misfortunes that could follow those events, but we, having lived through the consequences of those events, know that the benefits went largely to Europe and America, or the colonising nations, and the misfortunes to Africa, or the colonised peoples. Where Smith wondered about the possible benefits and misfortunes, Marx and Engels were clear that arising from the dialectically linked benefits and misfortunes of capitalist modernity was the creation of the world that reflected the West. In making all nations on pain of extinction to partake of that modernity, "it compels them to introduce what it calls civilisation into their midst ... In one word, it creates a world after its own image".[8] The creation of a world after the image of the Western bourgeoisie was not without resistance – as seen in class and national struggles everywhere.

Because of its historical constitution, South Africa was to embody more intensely than most the consequences of the benefits (to a white minority linked to Europe) and the misfortunes, to the majority linked to the rest of Africa and Asia, with the minority trying to create a South Africa after its own image, which it also saw as representative of what it called Western civilisation. But South Africa was also to embody the resistance against the negative consequences of that modernity, and in its history we see the clashes and interactions of race, class, gender, ethnicity, religion and the social forces that bedevil the world today.

Thus, South Africa as the site of concentration of both domination and resistance was to mirror the worldwide struggles between capital and labour, and between the colonising and the colonised. For Africa, let's face it, South African history, from Vasco da Gama's landing at the Cape in 1498 to its liberation in 1994, frames all modern social struggles, certainly black struggles. If the struggle, often fought out with swords, between racialised capital and racialised labour was about wealth and power, it was also a battle over image, often fought out with words, and when Biko asserts the right to "write what I like", he is asserting the right to draw the image of himself, unfettered – a position reflective of Robert Sobukwe. Images are very important. You have seen how we all like looking at ourselves in the mirror. We all like to have our photos taken. In many African societies, the shadow is thought to carry the soul of a person. But here we are talking about the image of the world as a physical, economic, political, moral and intellectual universe of our being. This image resides in the memory. So, also, are dreams. So, also, our concept of life.

Colonialism tried to control the memory of the colonised, or rather – to borrow from the Caribbean thinker, Sylvia Wynter – it tried to subject the colonised to its memory, to make the colonised see themselves through the hegemonic memory of the colonising centre.[9] Put another way, the colonising presence tried to mutilate the memory of the colonised and, where that failed, it dismembered it, and then tried to remember it to the coloniser's memory: his way of defining the world, including his take on the nature of the relations between the coloniser and the colonised.

This relation was primarily economic, for nobody colonises another for the aesthetic joy of simply doing it. The colonised as worker, as peasant, produces for another. His land and his labour benefit another. This is, of course, effected through power, political power, but it is also accomplished through cultural subjugation, the control of the entire education system for instance, the ultimate goal being to establish psychic dominance on the part of the coloniser and psychic submission on the part of the colonised.

Economic and political subjugation are obvious, for you cannot convince a person who has lost his land to forget the loss; the person who goes hungry, to forget his hunger; and the person who bears the whiplashes of an unjust system, to forget the pain. But cultural subjugation is more dangerous, because it is more subtle and its effects long-lasting. Moreover, it can make a person who has lost his land, who feels the pangs of hunger, who carries flagellated flesh, look at those experiences differently. For instance, from the standpoint of pessimism, "oh there is nothing I can do about this", failing to see in his history any positive lessons in his dealings with the present. He or she has been drained of historical memory of a different world. The prophet who once warned, "fear not those who kill the body but those who kill the spirit", was right on the mark; and Steve Biko with his Black Consciousness was working within the prophetic warning.

Consciousness distinguishes humans from the rest of nature. In humans, death is marked by the end of consciousness. In that sense, all humans, to the extent that they are human, have a consciousness. But in a situation of the coloniser and the colonised, the question of consciousness is vital; in fact, it becomes a site of intense struggle. Let me fall back on Hegel. In his books, particularly in *Phenomenology of the Spirit* and *Science of Logic,* Hegel distinguishes Being-in-itself (not the Kantian unknowable thing-in-itself) and Being-for-itself.[10] Being-in-itself is mere existence. Being-for-itself is being aware not only of its existence, but existence for a purpose, an ethical purpose, the distinction illustrated by the saying: "I live to eat and I eat to live". But in a situation of the master and the slave, the for-itself can be appropriated by another, to become the for-another. Marx was to apply the same notion for classes and class struggle, distinguishing between a class-in-itself, and a class-for-itself, when it becomes aware of itself as a class with its own class interests and identity. The struggle of classes takes the form of the dominant trying to turn the dominated class not into a class for itself, but a class for the interests of another, the dominating. In race politics, the same can apply when the self-consciousness of a race is appropriated by another to serve the interests of a dominant race.

Racism was a conscious class ideology of imperialism; and colonialism and colonial relations, even then clearly economic and political, often came wrapped in race. The problem of the twentieth century, said du Bois, was that of the colour line, "the relation of the darker to the lighter races of men in Asia and Africa, in America and the islands of the sea."[11] The more class-conscious CLR James was to add that while the race question was subsidiary to the class question in politics, and that to think of imperialism in terms of race was disastrous, "to neglect the racial factor as merely incidental is an error only less grave than to make it fundamental."[12] Within the overall context of economic and political domination, race could be, was and is often used as a means of diminishing the self-evaluation of the dominated. In that context, racial self-assertion was a necessary first step in the reclamation of a positive self-awareness. A person without a consciousness of his Being in the World, to use the Heideggardian phrase, is lost and can easily be guided by another to wherever the guide wants to take him, even to his own extinction.

Black Consciousness, then, becomes the right of black peoples to draw an image of themselves that negates and transcends the image of themselves that was drawn by those who would weaken them in their fight for and assertion of their humanity. Or, in the Sobukwe era, formulation to fight for the right to call our souls our own. It seeks to draw the image of a possible world, different and transcending the one drawn by the West, by reconnecting itself to a different historical memory and dreams, and that is why in a preface to the 1996 edition of Biko's book, *I Write What I Like,* Bishop Tutu makes a tantalising connection between consciousness and renaissance. "It is good that there is this new edition to enable us to savour the inspired words of Steve Biko – perhaps it could just spark a black renaissance."[13] Here Tutu intimates that positive self-consciousness can open new vistas and extensions of our being, but consciousness resides in memory.

Even at the very simple level of our daily experience, we get excited when we visit, say, the place we were born, and recall the various landmarks of our childhood. Sometimes we feel a sense of loss when we find that the place no longer holds any traces of what it once meant to us. Memory is also the site of dreams, desire. And when we say that a person has lost his or her memory, we are talking of a real loss of those traces that individuals use to make sense of what is happening to them. Imprisonment and torture alter or break memory.

If the site of dreams, desire, image and consciousness is memory, then where is the location of memory itself? What is the site of memory? Memory lies in language. In incorporating the colonial world into the international capitalist order and relations with itself as the centre of that order and those relations, the imperialist West also went about subjecting the rest of the world to its memory through a vast naming system. It planted its memory on our landscape by renaming it. *Egoli* or whatever was the original name, becomes Johannesburg. The great East African Lake, known by the Luo people as Namlolwe, becomes Lake Victoria. They also planted their memory on our bodies. Ngugi becomes James. Noliwe becomes Margaret. Our names get stuck with their names. Thus our bodies, in terms of their self-definition, become forever branded by their memory.

The name mark pointing to my body defines my identity. James? And I answer, "Yes. I am". And, most important, they planted their memory on our intellect through language. Language and the culture it carries is the most crucial part of that naming system by which Europe subjected the colonised to its memory. The more educated in the culture of the coloniser, the more severe the subjection, with devastating results for the colonial subject as a whole.

Writers, artists, musicians, intellectuals, workers in ideas are the keepers of memory of a community. What fate awaits a community when its keepers of memory have been subjected to the West's linguistic means of production and storage of memory – English, French and Portuguese – so that those who should have been keepers of the sacred word can now only see themselves and the different possibilities for the community within the linguistic boundaries of memory incorporated? We have languages but our keepers of memory feel that they cannot store knowledge, emotions, intellect, in African languages.

It is like having a granary, but at harvest you store your produce in somebody else's granary. The result is that ninety per cent of intellectual production in Africa is stored in European languages, a continuation of the colonial project where not even a single treaty between Europe and Africa exists in any African language. We do not exist in these languages!

The relationship between African and European languages as producers and storers of memory has been at the heart of the struggle for a sovereign consciousness. It has certainly been part of the South African intellectual tradition, at least since the rise of what scholar Ntongela Masilela calls the New African Movement. Let me quote two instances:

In *The South African Outlook* of 1 July 1939, there is a letter to the editor written by BW Vilakazi. It is a reply to his friend and fellow writer, HIE Dhlomo, the younger of the two Dhlomos. HIE Dhlomo wrote in English as opposed to his elder brother RRR Dhlomo who wrote in

Zulu. HIE Dhlomo had published an article on African drama and poetry in which he disagreed with Vilakazi's MA thesis, "The Conception and Development of Poetry in Zulu". Where Dhlomo draws from Hebrew and Shakespeare and quotes liberally from Western sources, including Sir Arthur Quiller Couch, to buttress his argument, Vilakazi turns the tables to remind Dhlomo that he does not write in Zulu. Vilakazi, aligning himself subtly with the elder Dhlomo, is clearly unapologetic in his building on the literary heritage of the Zulu language in form and content.

"My course primarily lies in Zulu poetry. And there I am definite. Zulu poetry is a contribution to Zulu literature. Secondly, I am convinced it is a mission, a self-imposed mission, to help build a vista of Bantu poetry. And Zulu poetry will therefore stand parallel to English, German or Italian poetry, all of which form the realm of what is called European poetry."[14]

In saying that Zulu is part of Bantu literature and that Bantu poetry stands on the same parallel as European poetry, Vilakazi is arguing that Zulu or any African language is to African Literature what any particular European language is to European literature. He recognises that there is no abstract African literature that is not rooted in specific African languages, any more than there is an abstract European literature that is not rooted in specific European languages. He is very clear as to what he means by Bantu literature: "By Bantu drama, I mean a drama written by a Bantu, for the Bantu, in a Bantu language. I do not class English or Afrikaans dramas on Bantu themes, whether [or not] these are written by black people. I do not call them contributions to Bantu literature. It is the same with poetry ... ".[15]

And then follows a statement that is really a celebration of his refusal to be subjected to the linguistic perimeters of European memory: "I have an unshaken belief in the possibilities of Bantu languages and their dramas, provided the Bantu writers themselves can learn to love their languages, and use them as vehicles for thought, feeling and will. After all, the belief, resulting in literature, is a demonstration of people's 'self' where they cry: *'Ego quad sum'.* That is our pride in being black and we cannot change creation."[16]

Is this not a literary expression of black consciousness long before Biko gave it a name and currency? Vilakazi's conscious commitment to African languages takes us back to Krune Mqhayi.

In his book, *Long Walk to Freedom,* Mandela describes an event in his school, Healdtown, that for him was "like a comet streaking across the night sky".[17] It was a visit by Krune Mqhayi. Performing on the stage in his native Xhosa dress and holding an assegai, he tells his mesmerised audience: "'The assegai stands for what is glorious and true in African history. It is a symbol of the African as a warrior and the African as artist'",[18] and contrasts this to the skilful but soulless Europe: "'What I am talking to you about is not … the overlapping of one culture over another. What I am talking about is the brutal clash between what is indigenous and good and what is foreign and bad … We cannot allow these foreigners who do not care for our culture to take over our nation. I predict that one day the forces of African society will achieve a momentous victory over the interloper'".[19]

The performance profoundly impacted the young Mandela's previous assumptions about white and black power. "I could hardly believe my ears. His boldness in speaking of such delicate matters in the presence of Dr Wellington and other whites seemed utterly astonishing to us. Yet, at the same time, it aroused and motivated us, and began to alter my perception of men like Dr Wellington whom I had considered as my benefactor".[20]

But Mqhayi's performance, with its unapologetic celebration of being both Xhosa and African, does something more: it shows that there is no such thing as an Abstract African and it makes the young Mandela accept his own Xhosa-Being as the real condition of his African-Being, and not the other way round. Mqhayi wrote in Xhosa, and in the *Bantu World* of 20 July 1935, the same year of the event narrated by Mandela, Guybon B Sinxo, another South African intellectual, wrote a commissioned piece on Mqhayi in which, among other tributes, he describes Mqhayi's book,

Ityala Lama Wele, as being next only to the Bible in greatness. And of Mqhayi, who learnt under the feet of Xhosa elders, he writes: "Today ... that same boy who, at a time when most of the educated Africans in the Cape as well as the Europeans controlling Native Education looked down upon Xhosa, stood up for our language, and by pen and word of mouth created a renaissance in our literature."[21]

The issue carries, in banner headlines devised by the sub-editor, RV Selope Thema, this tribute to Mqhayi as a creator of Xhosa renaissance.

What stands out, on looking back, is not only this wholehearted tribute by two fellow intellectuals, Sinxo, a Xhosa, and Thema, a Pedi, but the fact that the term "renaissance" is used in 1935 in reference to the work of an African intellectual who wrote in an African language and whose performance in that language had such a profound impact on the Healdtown students. From their tributes, Mqhayi emerges as a renaissance figure combining in himself many talents and interests: an *imbongi*, performer, writer, poet, dramatist, essayist, translator, humorist, critic, cultural advocate, political analyst; a public intellectual who preaches and practises his doctrine. Are there echoes of this renaissance when years later in 1994, Mandela exhorts Africa to believe in itself? "We know it is a matter of fact that we have it in ourselves as Africans to change all this. We must, in action, say that there is no obstacle big enough to stop us from bringing about a new African Renaissance."[22]

Since the 1994 call, Thabo Mbeki has further elaborated on this theme and his 1996 address, "I am an African", with its poetic suggestiveness, its depiction of this "African" as containing in himself multitudes, a truly renaissance persona, has justifiably become a classic. Clearly, the African Renaissance seems to be an idea whose time has come, to witness the number of books, articles and conferences which it has generated. The discussions have been rich in their economic, political and even cultural exploration of meaning and implications of the idea. However, the shortcomings in the recent academic discussions, as opposed to those of the times of Mqhayi and Vilakazi, have been a virtual silence over the relationship between language and renaissance. Language, though often seen as a product and reflection of economic, political and cultural order, is itself a material force of the highest order.

That is why we must ask: is an African Renaissance possible when we, the keepers of memory, have to work outside our own linguistic memory? Working within the prison house of European linguistic memory? Often drawing from our own experiences and history to enrich the already very rich European memory?

Bothered by our almost religious attachment to that memory, Cheikh Anito Diop, another multi-talented figure in the Mqhayi tradition, in 1948 posed the same question in a paper published in *Le Musée Vivant* under the title, "When can we talk of an African Renaissance?" After reviewing the predicament and even the complexity of Africans writing in European languages, he ends up echoing Vilakazi's sentiments in very emphatic terms, in fact asserting that: "It is absolutely indispensable to destroy this attachment to the prestige of European languages in the greater interest of Africa".[23]

Some could raise the objection that Africans who use foreign languages do so in an original manner and that their expression contains something specific to their race. But what the African can never express, until he abandons the use of foreign languages, is the peculiar genius of his own languages ... all these reasons – and more – lead me into affirming that the development of our languages is the prerequisite for a real African Renaissance.

Nadine Gordimer was to express similar sentiments in her contribution to a United Nations Educational, Scientific and Cultural Organisation (Unesco) symposium in Harare in 1992. In the paper called "Turning the Page: African Writers in the Twenty-first Century", she, of course, acknowledges, and rightly so, the brilliance of what has already been produced by African writers in acquired European tongues and then adds: "But we writers cannot speak of taking up the challenge of a new century for African literature unless writing in African languages becomes the major component of the continent's literature. Without this, one cannot speak of an African literature. It must be the basis of the cultural cross-currents that will both buffer and stimulate that literature".[24]

What Diop and Gordimer say about literature applies to intellectual production as a whole, for renaissance is not about literature alone; it is exploration of the frontiers in the whole realm of economy, politics, science, arts, the extension of dreams and imagination.

Still, the quest for knowledge is central in the enterprise.

European renaissance involved not only the exploration of new frontiers of thought, but also a reconnection with their memory, with roots in ancient Greece and Rome. In practice, it meant a disengagement from the tyranny of hegemonic Latin and the discovery of their own tongues. But it also meant a massive and sustained translation and transfer of knowledge from Latin and Greek into the emerging European vernaculars, including English. There was also a lot of inter-vernacular translation of current intellectual production among the then emerging European languages, for instance, from French into English and vice versa.

The African keepers of memory could do worse than usefully borrow a leaf from that experience. Thabo Mbeki's contribution to the debate, in fact, comes as a challenge to the African intelligentsia, the keepers of memory, to "add to the strengthening of the movement for Africa's renaissance".[25]

The challenge to the intelligentsia is as it should be. No renaissance can come out of state legislation and admonitions. States and governments can and should and must provide an enabling democratic environment and resources. In this respect, South Africa has to be commended for coming up with a very enlightened language policy. Most governments tend to hide their heads in the sand and pretend that African languages do not exist or else try to force a retrograde policy of monolingualism. Governments can help with policies that make African languages part of the languages of social mobility and power, currently a monopoly of European languages. But renaissance, as rebirth and flowering, can only spring from the wealth of imagination of the people, and above all, from its keepers of memory.

We must hearken to Diop's and Vilakazi's call when they tell us to use our languages as vehicles for "thought, feeling and will". We must produce knowledge in African languages and then use translation as a means of conversation in and among African languages. We must also translate from European and Asian languages into our own, for our languages must not stay isolated from the mainstream of progressive human thought in the languages and cultures of the globe.

But how can we change our present predicament, where a lot of knowledge produced by sons and daughters of Africa is already stored in European linguistic granaries? Many of these works, as Gordimer has noted, are brilliant examples of the results of acquisition of European languages. Diop makes the point over and over again that he is not underestimating the contributions by those African writers who use foreign languages. And Vilakazi, in his debate with HIE Dhlomo, is not questioning the quality of Dhlomo's work. These works, like stolen gems, must be retrieved and returned to the languages and cultures that inspired them in the first instance. The task of restoration is at the heart of the "Renaissance Project".

The problem and the process on a worldwide scale is what we at the International Centre for Writing and Translation at the University of California Irvine have dubbed the "Restoration Project".

What is the Restoration Project? As in Africa, a lot of the intellectual production by the native keepers of memory in Asia, the Pacific and within North American Native populations, has been in languages other than the ones spoken by the people. In reality, this is often an act of cultural translation from the subject memory into the dominant memory. But it is a mental act, which means that in the process, the original text is lost. The Restoration Project imagined at the International Centre for Writing and Translation, of which I am the first director, involves the support for models of translations for works written in dominant languages by people who draw from languages and cultures other than the dominant one, in which the works were first written. We call it a project of restoration because, in putting works back into the original languages (or into other marginalised languages as well), it would be helping to restore the work to its original language and culture without interfering in its existence in the dominant memory – almost like rescuing "the original" mental text from exile. Or, to use the metaphor of a harvest stored in somebody else's granary, it would be like the owners of the harvest retrieving their produce and restoring it in their granaries.

Conceived as a global project, it would affect quite a number of cultures in Asia, Africa, Europe and the islands, and it would help in redrawing the cultural power map of the world. For it is like reversing the brain drain by ensuring that the products of that brain drain go back to build the local base. The success of such restoration would have to be a creative partnership of the writer, the translator and publisher, and, of course, the state, which would provide an enabling economic and political environment. In such a situation, and given the place that, say, English occupies in the world today, no matter what we think of the process by which it came to occupy that position, we can challenge it to enable and not disable, use it to enable conversation among languages where, given the shortage of people who know two marginalised languages sufficiently for them to translate directly, we can use English or French as a medium to enable without disabling.

Once again, South Africa offers rich soil for a starting point or a model of such a global project. A very important work on the New African Movement has been done by the South African scholar, Ntongela Masilela. He has dug up old newspapers and come up with astonishing results of the enormous output of South African intellectuals of the 1920s, '30s and '40s, a good number of whom wrote and published in African languages. We would like to explore ways in which we can work with South African and international publishers to start a pilot project to have their unpublished works republished in book form, or those out of print reissued in scholarly editions in both the original African languages and in English. We would like to see, for instance, all the Zulu works of Mazisi Kunene, an intellectual descendant of Vilakazi, and the great tradition of Zulu orature going back to Magolwane and Mshongweni of Shaka's court, published in Zulu and other African languages. So too the historical Zulu novels of RRR Dhlomo. We would also like to see the works written in English by say, HIE Dhlomo, and others restored back to their original language and even other African languages. As I said, this is only a pilot model for what should be a global restoration project.

For us in Africa, and in the current ideas of renaissance, this can be a model for practical steps in realising the goals of the African Renaissance. We have, for instance, three Nobel Prize winners in Literature: Soyinka, Gordimer and Mafouz. Why shouldn't their works be made available in the languages and cultures of the continent which nourished their imagination? Why shouldn't the work of Biko be available in African languages? What about Nkrumah's, Nyerere's, Mandela's, Machel's, Neto's, Cheikh Anita Diop's work? What of all the corpus/oeuvres of all the African intellectuals? What of all the works of diasporic Africans in the Caribbean and Americas, Sonia Sanchez's, for instance? What of the works of the two other black Nobel winners, Derek Walcott and Toni Morrison? If we can think of scouting European museums asking and even demanding the return of our precious works of art, why not also the restoration of the precious works of written thought?

All this calls for a very different attitude and relationship to our languages on the part of African governments and the African intelligentsia as once articulated by Vilakazi, and Diop, and exemplified by Mqhayi and the whole line of African intellectuals who have always kept faith in African languages. There are signs of positive responses to his call.

Some governments have begun to come up with positive policies on African languages, the prime example once again being South Africa. There are a few countries, Ethiopia for instance, where writing and intellectual production in African languages has always been taken as the norm. The government's attitude to culture in general, and to African languages in particular, is important, for as Gordimer has rightly observed, "in the twentieth century of political struggles, state money has gone into guns, not books. As for literacy, as long as people can read state decrees and the graffiti that defies them, that has been regarded as sufficient proficiency".[26]

That, of course, is decidedly not the best recipe for a renaissance. The state can provide an enabling environment, including ensuring respect and protection of what Gordimer calls the implicit role of writers supplying a critique of society for the greater understanding and enrichment of life there. But ultimately, the work of intellectual rejuvenation must come from the keepers of memory, and here too there have been encouraging signs.

In January 2000, scholars who gathered in Asmara from all the regions of Africa and abroad, came up with the Asmara Declaration which called on African languages to accept the challenge, the duty and the responsibility of speaking for the continent. The second such conference is scheduled to be held in South Africa, and the Buwa regional conference next week is part of that dialogue and preparation for the second continental conference on the matter.

These trends are in keeping with what seems to me the main challenge of Biko's life, thought and legacy: to disengage ourselves from the tyranny of the European post-renaissance memory and seize back the right and the initiative to name the world by reconnecting to our memory. This brings us back to the words of the great African sage who, as he stood in Tunis hearing in his mind the words of the Roman general who sentenced the African city of Carthage to death, refused to moan about the death and past loss, but instead, he let its memory carry him on new waves of optimism. "All human civilisation rests on the foundation of the ruins such as those of the African city of Carthage",[27] Mandela said, recalling no doubt all the ruins wrought on the psyche of the continent by the more contemporary empires of European modernity. Then he issued the call: "One epoch with its historic task has come to an end. Surely another must commence with its own challenges. Africa cries out for a new birth. Carthage awaits the restoration of its glory".[28]

Surely, with his life, Nelson Mandela has earned the right to issue that call to the youth of Africa?

Biko would have understood that call. His life and thought, as that of Chris Hani, Robert Sobukwe, Ruth First, all the political prisoners and many others, remind us that whatever has been gained, including independence and national liberation, did not come of themselves. They were the results of struggle and sacrifice, and it behoves us, the inheritors of any and every benefit of those sacrifices, never to forget. A people without memory is in danger of losing its soul.

Is the task in front of us – that of the recovery of the African historical memory and dreams – too difficult a task? There is no way out of this. Keepers of African memory must do for their languages what all others in history have done for theirs. As we set about disengaging from the hegemonic tyranny of bourgeois Western memory and reconnecting with that contained in the living matter of our languages, let the words of Thabo Mbeki echo determination in our hearts and not waver in our resolve: "Whoever we may be, whatever our immediate interest, however much we carry baggage from our past, however much we have been caught by the fashion of cynicism and loss of faith in the capacity of the people, let us err today and say: nothing can stop us now."[29]

Among writers that Biko admired was Aimé Cesaire, whose poem, 'Return to my Native Land', is a poetic call and celebration, a return to the source of one's being, a vital reconnection with memory. The poem sums up the essence of Black Consciousness with a rejection and affirmation:

For it is not true that the work of man is finished.
That man has nothing more to do in the world
But be a parasite in the world
That all we now need is to keep in step with the world
But the work of man is only just beginning
And it remains to man to conquer all the violence
embedded in the recesses of his passion And no race
possesses the monopoly of beauty,
of intelligence, of freedom
There is a place for all at the rendezvous of victory.[30]

We can add to this and say that no language has a monopoly of beauty, that all memories have a place at the rendezvous of human victory.

Notes

1 Nelson Mandela. 1994. Address to the Organisation of African Unity (OAU). Tunis.
2 Steve Biko. 2004 [1978]. *I Write What I Like*. Johannesburg: Picador Africa, p. 192.
3 Nelson Mandela. 20 April 1964. Statement delivered at the Rivonia Trial. Pretoria.
4 Steve Biko. Unknown source.
5 Robert Sobukwe. Unknown source.
6 Thabo Mbeki. 1996. Address to the Constitutional Assembly of South Africa. Pretoria.
7 Friedrich Engels and Karl Marx. 2002 [1848]. *The Communist Manifesto*. London: Penguin Classics.
8 Engels and Marx, *The Communist Manifesto*.
9 Sylvia Wynter. Unknown source.
10 See Georg Wilhelm Friedrich Hegel (translated by AV Miller). 1977. *Phenomenology of the Spirit*. Oxford: Clarendon Press; and Georg Wilhelm Friedrich Hegel. 2004 [1890]. *Science of Logic*. New York: Routledge.
11 William Edward Burghardt du Bois. 1903. *The Souls of Black Folk*. New York: New American Library.
12 Cyril Lionel Robert James. 1989 [1938]. *The Black Jacobins: Toussaint L'Ouverture and the San Domingo Revolution*. New York: Vintage Press, p. 283.
13 Archbishop Emeritus Desmond Tutu. 1996. In Steve Biko. *I Write What I Like*. Johannesburg: Ravan Press, p. 10.
14 Benedict Vilikazi. 1 July 1939. Letter to the Editor. *The South African Outlook*.
15 Vilikazi, *The South African Outlook*.
16 Vilikazi, *The South African Outlook*.
17 Nelson Mandela. 1991. *A Long Walk to Freedom*. Johannesburg: Penguin Books.
18 Krune Mqhayi. In Mandela, *A Long Walk to Freedom*.
19 Mqhayi. In Mandela, *A Long Walk to Freedom*.
20 Mandela, *A Long Walk to Freedom*.
21 Guybon Sinxo. 20 July 1935. "Notable Contributions to Xhosa Literature: Mr. Mqhayi Creates Xhosa Renaissance". *Bantu World*.
22 Nelson Mandela. 10 May 1994. Statement of the President of the ANC Nelson Rolihlahla Mandela at his Inauguration as President of the Democratic Republic of South Africa. Pretoria. See www.anc.org.za/ancdocs/speeches/inaugpta.html (accessed 11 June 2009).
23 Cheikh Anito Diop. 1948. "When Can we Talk of an African Renaissance?" *Le Musée Vivant*.

24 Nadine Gordimer. 1992. "Turning the Page: African Writers in the Twenty-First Century". Address at a UNESCO symposium. Harare.
25 Thabo Mbeki. 28 September 1998. Statement by the then-Deputy President of the Republic of South Africa at the African Renaissance Conference. Johannesburg. See www.anc.org.za/ancdocs/history/mbeki/1998/tm0928.htm (accessed 11 June 2009).
26 Gordimer, "Turning the Page".
27 Mandela, Address to the OAU.
28 Mandela, Address to the OAU.
29 Thabo Mbeki. 8 May 1996. Statement of then-Deputy President Thabo Mbeki on behalf of the African National Congress on the occasion of the adoption by the Constitutional Assembly of The Republic of South Africa Constitution Bill 1996. Cape Town. See www.anc.org.za/ancdocs/history/mbeki/1996/sp960508.html (accessed 11 June 2009).
30 Aimé Césaire. 1969. *Return to my Native Land*. Paris: Présence Africaine.

5

Ten Years of Democracy: 1994–2004

Speaker: Former President Nelson Mandela
Date: 10 September 2004

"History, from time to time, brings to the fore the kind of leaders who seize the moment, who cohere the wishes and aspirations of the oppressed. Such was Steve Biko, a fitting product of his time; a proud representative of the reawakening of a people."

– *Nelson Mandela*

Ten Years of Democracy: 1994–2004

Chancellor, Vice-Chancellor, Dr Mangcu, distinguished guests, ladies and gentlemen: Thank you for inviting us to deliver this annual lecture in the name of one of the great heroes in the struggle for the liberation of our country, Steve Bantu Biko.

We are deeply honoured to be thus associated with a South African and African whom we were forced by circumstance and history to observe from a distance, from the confines of a prison, as he lived out his brief but so powerful and evocative presence on the political landscape of this country.

His death, which we remember and commemorate in these days, was in many ways as powerful in its effect on our national consciousness as was his life.

From Robben Island we followed with immense interest the movement led and inspired by Steve Biko. Our views on the Black Consciousness Movement at the time have been published and are part of public record.

The driving thrust of Black Consciousness was to forge pride and unity amongst all the oppressed, to foil the strategy of divide-and-rule, to engender pride amongst the mass of our people and confidence in their ability to throw off their oppression.

For its part, the ANC welcomed Black Consciousness as part of the genuine forces of the revolution. We understood that it was helping to give organisational form to the popular upsurge of all the oppressed groups of our society. Above all, the liberation movement asserted that in struggle – whether in mass action, underground organisation, armed actions or international mobilisation – the people would most readily develop consciousness of their proud being, of their equality with everyone else, of their capacity to make history.

And, as we now increasingly speak of and work for an African

Renaissance, the life, work, words, thoughts and example of Steve Biko assume a relevance and resonance as strong as in the time that he lived. His revolution had a simple but overwhelmingly powerful dimension in which it played itself out – that of radically changing the consciousness of people. The African Renaissance calls for and is situated in exactly such a fundamental change of consciousness: consciousness of ourselves, our place in the world, our capacity to shape history, and our relationship with each other and the rest of humanity.

The intervention on the level of consciousness – and consciousness was a key concept in his political approach and vocabulary – was at the essence of Biko's strategic brilliance and understanding. That intervention came at a time when the political pulse of our people had been rendered faint by banning, imprisonment, exile, murder and banishment. Repression had swept the country clear of all visible organisation of the people. But it was also a time when the tide of Africa's valiant struggle and her liberation, lapping at our own borders, was consolidating black pride across the world and firing the determination of all those who were oppressed to take their destiny into their own hands.

History, from time to time, brings to the fore the kind of leaders who seize the moment, who cohere the wishes and aspirations of the oppressed. Such was Steve Biko, a fitting product of his time; a proud representative of the reawakening of a people.

We may benefit greatly from again reflecting upon the role and power of consciousness, as understood by Biko, in the development and shaping of the quality of a society.

We South Africans have succeeded quite admirably in putting in place policies, structures, processes and implementation procedures for the transformation and development of our country. We are widely recognised and praised for having one of the most progressive constitutions in the world. The solidity of our democratic order, with all of its democracy-supporting structures and institutions, is beyond doubt. Our economic framework is sound and we are steadily making progress in bringing basic services to more and more of our people. It is at the level of what we once referred to as the RDP of the soul, that we as a nation and people might have crucially fallen behind since the attainment of democracy. The values of human solidarity that once drove our quest for a humane society seem to have been replaced, or are being threatened, by a crass materialism and pursuit of social goals of instant gratification. One of the challenges of our time, without being pietistic or moralistic, is to re-instil in the consciousness of our people that sense of human solidarity, of being in the world for one another and because of and through others. It is, as Biko did at that particular moment in history, to excite the consciousness of people with the humane possibilities of change.

"In time," he said then, "... we shall be in a position to bestow upon South Africa the greatest gift possible – a more human face."[1] And he inspired an emerging generation to take faith in that assertion and possibility. Faith in the possibility of building a qualitatively better world asks to be rekindled. It is the unflinching adherence to that kind of faith that distinguished the other great African patriot you asked me to remember in this talk tonight – Oliver Tambo.

I am often deeply under the impression of how our celebration of the not-inconsiderable achievements of democratic South Africa tends to focus on the contributions and roles of such as Mandela and Mbeki – who had the privilege of being founding presidents – and others who enjoyed prominence during the transitional negotiations. And as a consequence, how often it is neglected to explicitly recognise and acknowledge the hand of him who was architect, foundation layer and builder of that which we today celebrate and enjoy.

I am therefore grateful to you for recognising Oliver Tambo in your invitation to us.

The story of Oliver's life spans many themes and is rich in its narrative. The one theme I wish to highlight this evening is his remarkable, and possibly unique, leadership triumph over the hardships of political exile. Few liberation movements in exile withstood those hardships and challenges in the manner the ANC did under the leadership of Oliver Tambo.

The banning of the ANC and other political organisations, the imprisonment of the leadership, the intensification of repression by the apartheid regime, all added up to a situation where the liberation movements were under extreme pressure. The movement had to gather and regroup in exile and conduct the struggle from foreign and unknown soil. Oliver was already sent abroad to head up the foreign mission of the organisation and it fell on his shoulders to lead the movement in exile.

It is remarkable to observe that the ANC today – nine decades after its formation – is stronger than it has ever been. Its support continues to grow and expand, and it has become the political home of South Africans from all backgrounds and sectors of society. That achievement is the direct continuation and culmination of the building, holding together, uniting and growing Tambo presided over and led in exile.

I was reminded at the time when we were approaching the end of our term as president, and people were anxiously or mischievously asking what happens after Mandela goes, how similar anxieties were expressed about what would happen after Chief Albert Luthuli.

Few, if any, of those observers considered or mentioned Oliver Tambo. Once more, a leader of vision stepped up to the historic moment, responding to the needs and desires of the oppressed. The history of South Africa could have been vastly different if Oliver Tambo had not provided the leadership he did at the time and in the circumstances.

The struggle against apartheid became one of the foremost moral struggles of the twentieth century. Like few other liberation struggles, it drew the support of people from the widest range of political persuasions across the world. It succeeded in mobilising the abhorrence of the entire humanity against the debasement of racism. Oliver Tambo was the tireless campaigner and spokesperson for this African cause that became a world cause. One of his supreme achievements on the world stage was to imprint indelibly on the international consciousness the cause of an African nation and of Africa.

We have proven in recent years, particularly through the actions and example of our president, that we are seriously engaged in the quest for and the advancement of African unity, and as part of that, our growing consciousness of the African diaspora. These developments in our understanding of ourselves and our place in the world are legacies of the work of Oliver Tambo who built those networks of friendship and solidarity from which he could launch our cause onto the broader international stage.

Today we are a nation at peace with itself, united in our diversity, not only proclaiming but living out the contention that South Africa belongs to all who live in it. We take our place amongst the nations of the world, confident and proud in being an African country. We would not have been here had it not been for the exceptionally gifted leadership of Oliver Tambo.

Thank you to the Steve Biko Foundation for the opportunity to remember my old friend, partner and comrade. And to participate in the honouring of the memory of Steve Biko.

I thank you.

Notes

1 Steve Biko. 2004 [1978]. *I Write What I Like*. Johannesburg: Picador Africa, p. 108.

6

Citizenship as Stewardship

Speaker: Dr Mamphela Ramphele
Date: 12 September 2005

"Bantu Stephen Biko's key contribution to the freedom we enjoy today is in freeing us from the fear of death, thus allowing us to become fully what we were created to be – agents of our own history."

– *Mamphela Ramphele*

Citizenship as Stewardship

It is good to be here. This is an occasion to celebrate a life lived fully and a gift of life given freely. Bantu Stephen Biko's key contribution to the freedom we enjoy today is in freeing us from the fear of death, thus allowing us to become fully what we were created to be – agents of our own history. By accepting our historical agency we are able to give to Africa, in his own words, "the greatest gift still possible – a more human face".[1]

My lecture focuses on citizenship as stewardship. I will explore the extent to which we have delivered on the promise of this "greatest gift of all" and thus honour the martyrs who made the ultimate sacrifice to enable us to enjoy the fruits of democracy today. The lecture will explore the meaning of citizenship as stewardship. It will link citizenship and ownership. It will pose questions about our performance as the stewards of this young democracy and suggest some ways of giving further practical effect to our commitments.

It is good to be here. We are privileged to be able to celebrate all the "martyrs of hope" throughout our long struggle for freedom. In particular, we salute the young people who gave their lives in their thousands from the 1970s to the 1990s so that we could enjoy the joys of citizenship that we have become accustomed to over the past eleven years.

It is good to be here to celebrate the many other sacrifices that have made us the proud nation we are today. The many poor people who made the Truth and Reconciliation Commission process a success, reopened their wounds to the world and generously forgave their tormentors, thereby forgoing the opportunity for retributive justice. The Guguletu Seven Mothers are a prime example of the generosity that purchased the peace we enjoy today. We should also pay tribute to the thousands of families in many parts of our country that lost loved ones in the bloody civil war preceding our political settlement. They paid the price that we risk devaluing by characterising our political transition as "a miracle". Miracles happen by divine intervention. Our transition is the blessed product of many sacrifices by ordinary men, women and children.

It is good to be here at an educational institution. We should not neglect to pay tribute to the many thousands of young people who sacrificed their youth and heeded the 1970/1980's call: "Freedom Now and Education Tomorrow". For many of them, that "tomorrow" has yet to come. The twenty-first century competitive knowledge-economy realities leave little room for unskilled people. Many of them are unemployed, marginalised and bewildered. What are we, as the custodians of the freedom they sacrificed for, going to do to extend opportunities for them to enter the "tomorrow" they dreamt of in the heyday of street battles?

It is good to be here at UCT; my alma mater remains a place close to my heart, a place that nurtured and stimulated me for more than sixteen years of my adult life. I am the richer for it. It is good to be here at the Jameson Hall – the prime ritual space of this great institution. It is a space that embodies the many contradictions of our history, the tears and joys of our struggle for freedom and the triumph of transcendence. That we have come to love the Jammie symbolises the triumph of good over evil.

It is good to be here. I feel privileged to have come back to this beloved country after my sojourn across the Atlantic. Absence does make the heart grow fonder. I do not mean this in the romantic sense only. I also intend to reflect the value of retreating from daily encounters as perfected by the spiritual desert fathers from ancient times to present day. Their retreat from daily toils allows them to enter into even deeper engagement with the challenges facing the communities they serve. I feel much more connected to my country than ever before. Distance has provided me with perspectives that close encounters and intimacy tend to put out of focus.

HOW ARE WE DOING THUS FAR?

We are doing very well for a democracy as young as we are. At eleven years old, we are no different from the proverbial teenager. Flexing our nascent muscles and asserting ourselves at home and abroad. We have much to be proud of. We have courageously tackled the enormous task of redressing the legacy of centuries of misrule, poor economic management and inequity. We have emerged from our political settlement talks with a proud foundation for our democracy, our National Constitution, that has served us well in setting policy and implementation parameters. We have reason to beam with pride at our performance thus far.

The government has to be commended for having successfully created a transformative national policy framework second to none, to tackle the ills of the legacy of inequity. We have a stable macro-economic framework that has taught us, for the first time in our history, to live within our means. We have a growing economy that is providing significant opportunities and lifting many out of poverty. We have a growing middle class that is fuelling demand for goods and services, thus propelling the economy to greater heights. We have progressive policies reflecting the commitments we made in enshrining socio-economic rights in our National Constitution. We have sensible *regstellende aksie* legislation to rectify the injustices of the past, such as promoting employment equity, gender equality, black economic empowerment, land reform, etc.

We have set ourselves very high standards as a nation. Given the gap between those high standards and the legacy we inherited, it is not surprising that we have under-performed in a number of important areas. There are still too many South Africans left behind in poverty, despair and powerlessness with little prospect of being heard.

There are still too many going to bed hungry. Too many people are still without jobs and the dignity of self-reliance. Too many children still suffer abuse and homelessness despite our commitment to the Rights of the Child. Too many women fall victim to violence, both physical and sexual, notwithstanding our vows to promote gender equality. Too many old people are abused and subject to misery and lonely deaths despite our rhetoric of *ubuntu*. Too many of our fellow citizens are dying needlessly from preventable and treatable diseases, particularly HIV/AIDS, despite our commitment to the Right to Health. Our inadequate human capital base is being further eroded by HIV/AIDS, which is stealing those in the prime of their lives and depriving children of motherly love. The gap between the haves and have-nots continues to grow despite our commitments to a better life for all.

Many of the problems that still beset our society could have been tackled over the first decade of our democracy. Contrary to critics who blame the government's Growth, Employment and Redistrilaution (GEAR) policy, we have the financial resources to address our challenges and provide for the basic needs of all our citizens. Every year since 1994, unspent funds have been returned to the fiscus instead of being applied for the purposes intended. What we seem to be lacking is the political will to close the gaps between the values we espouse and our daily practices; between policy-making and implementation; between problem analysis and strategic interventions.

A key constraint to closing these gaps seems to be our failure to acknowledge and address human and intellectual capital weaknesses in a systematic and consistent manner. We spent too much time post-1994 in denial about the extent to which apartheid education had damaged our skills base. It was as if we feared that acknowledgement of our woundedness would be interpreted as proof that we were indeed of inferior intellect, as asserted by racists, and unready to govern. Our denial betrayed our vulnerability to buying into racist myths that confuse lack of knowledge with low intelligence. It is refreshing to see the growing candour from government in acknowledging the seriousness of our human capital challenges. For example, a recent government survey found that only eight per cent of people in key jobs at the local authority level of government have the requisite skills to do the jobs they hold.

This explains much of the failure to deliver services where it matters most – where people live.

It is not surprising that the government has become a prime target of criticism for these failures. This is understandable given the responsibilities that the government bears for creating an enabling climate for delivery on the promises of freedom. But is it fair to put the blame for past and present failures only at the doorstep of government? Is government alone to blame for our failure to make freedom a reality for those at the bottom of the socio-economic pyramid?

A Native American leader, Polingaysi Qoyawayma, in 1964, had this to say about accepting criticism: "No one likes to be criticised but criticism can be something like the desert wind that, in whipping the tender stalks, forces them to strike their roots down deeper for security."[2] We have to be courageous enough to accept criticism. Even better, we have to develop the capacity for self-criticism so that the roots of our tender democracy can be driven even deeper.

TAKING OWNERSHIP

Who is responsible for this under-performance? We have to own both our successes and our failures. Let us remember the commitments we made in adopting our Constitution. We boldly stated in the preamble that: "We, the people of South Africa, recognise the injustices of our past; honour those who suffered for justice and freedom in our land; respect those who have worked to build and develop our country; and believe that South Africa belongs to all who live in it, united in our diversity. We, therefore, through our freely elected representatives, adopt this Constitution as the supreme law of the Republic so as to heal the divisions of the past and establish a society based on democratic values, social justice and fundamental human rights; lay the foundations for a democratic and open society in which government is based on the will of the people and every citizen is equally protected by law; improve the quality of life of all citizens and free the potential of each person;

and build a united and democratic South Africa able to take its rightful place as a sovereign state in the family of nations."³

This preamble is testimony to our acceptance that our citizenship is an active one. We accepted both the rights bestowed on us by our Constitution, and the responsibilities attached to being citizens. Citizenship is about ownership. The Afrikaans word *burgers* captures the spirit of ownership better. *Burgers,* over the ages, took their ownership of the land as sacred. They accepted the duties of *burgerskap* willingly. They saw themselves as guardians of the land they inherited. They exercised their guardianship to honour those who had gone before them, to sustain the livelihoods of those who depended on them in the present, and to ensure that future generations would continue to enjoy the rights and privileges the land provided them.

Citizenship as stewardship is about taking ownership of the gift of freedom. Stewardship is defined as the mantle under which all progressive causes operate: human rights, conservation, economic welfare, government reform and over-sight, education, health care, disaster relief, animal welfare, mental health and peace. Stewardship is about meeting the obligations we willingly committed to in our Constitution.

As citizens of our young democracy we have a sacred duty of care. Andrew Shepherd, as quoted in *The American President* by Aaron Sorkin, captures this duty aptly: "You want to claim this land as the land of the free? The symbol of your country cannot just be a flag. The symbol also has to be of its citizen exercising his right to burn the flag in protest. Now show me that, defend that, celebrate that in your classrooms. Then you can sing about the land of the free."⁴

The question facing us today is the extent to which we can demonstrate that we have indeed gone beyond the symbols of our citizenship, be they the flag, the national anthem or the values enshrined in our Constitution. Have we gone beyond singing about our beloved country to defending its values by living them out in our daily lives in the classrooms, the boardrooms, the office complex, the factory floor, the hospital ward, the police station, or any other space where we are active as citizens?

South Africa has traditionally exhibited different understandings of citizenship. Two main variants of citizenship dominated our pre-1994 landscape: republican and liberal. Republican citizenship emphasises self-governance and active participation in the affairs of state as a sacred duty. Many adherents of the republican view of citizenship either defended, or worked actively in opposition to the injustices of apartheid. Liberal citizenship emphasises individual rights and government accountability. In this view of citizenship, the responsibilities and obligations of the individual citizen take a back seat as each pursues what they see as being in their best interest. During the long struggle for freedom, many white South Africans took the liberal view of citizenship to the extreme. They became passive beneficiaries of a system that protected their material interests whilst pleading powerlessness to influence the direction the society was taking.

Black South Africans who were excluded from citizenship rights then, face the challenge of defining what citizenship means to them today. I would like to suggest that all of us as South Africans, black and white, need to face up to the challenge of revisiting the idea of citizenship, and critically evaluate our performance against the stewardship role we accepted in the new democratic order.

KEY PERFORMANCE AREAS

Failure to take ownership of our democracy is evident in many areas of our society. First, many citizens complain that they are not being taken seriously as voters. They resent being used as vote fodder by political parties, only to be discarded as soon as political positions are secured by the few. The system of proportional representation has not helped in attaching a face to a vote to enable voters to hold that person accountable for delivery on election promises. It is, however, not sufficient for citizens to adopt a cynical view to elections and neglect their responsibilities to demand more accountability from elected officials. The vote is a powerful tool that should be used strategically to express approval or disapproval of those entrusted with public office.

Second, the idea of civil service as an opportunity to serve seems to have become overshadowed by the notion of civil service as a job opportunity for the individual involved. The wisdom embedded in the idea that, "in serving each other, we become free"[5], as William Nicholson put it in a website on metaphors of stewardship, is lost on the many civil servants who fail to pass the test of common courtesy to citizens who are entitled to public services. Some of the officials behave no differently from their apartheid predecessors in treating their fellow citizens with disrespect. Could it be that some of our civil servants have yet to take delivery of the freedom that would have made them recognise the sacred duty of serving their fellow citizens with dignity? Could it also be that the linkage of service with subservience for the majority of poor black people in the bad apartheid years has damaged the capacity for service in some people in the civil service of the new democracy? Whatever the reason, it is not acceptable for civil servants to expect taxpayers to continue to pay them for the privilege to be insulted.

The government, for its part, needs to set and enforce the parameters for accountability. Party loyalty is not a sufficient basis for appointment to public service. The appalling skills gaps in the civil service, as well as the unsustainable vacancy rates, reflect not only lack of skills, but the corroding impact of politicisation of appointments at many levels of our civil service. There are too many skilled professionals being denied job opportunities at the various levels of government because they are outside the party political networks that have captured civil service jobs for patronage.

Comparative analyses worldwide point to the importance of limiting political appointments based on loyalty only to the top layer. Strict professional competency criteria need to be applied for the rest of the system to ensure efficiency and effectiveness. We need to strengthen professional recruitment, promotion, training and retraining of public officials at all levels of government. No longer can we tolerate municipal managers who lack basic management skills and the capacity to co-ordinate and give leadership to tackling the complex demands of running cities and towns. Mediocrity has to be rooted out and meritocracy promoted. We run a serious risk of losing even more of our brightest skilled people for greener pastures where their value is more appreciated. We stand to lose the competition for skills in today's global knowledge economy if we do not rise to the challenge of retraining those we train at great cost.

Third, professionalism is a matter of pride and a mark of maturity. Have we as a nation sufficiently signified our respect for and appreciation of professionalism in our public service? How does one explain the widespread unprofessionalism that plagues our public institutions? What has become of the pride that nurses had in neat uniforms, tidy wards, comforted patients and, above all, a sense of purpose in being part of the healing profession? What has become of the pride of place teachers enjoyed in the lives of communities everywhere, including during the bad apartheid years? How do we continue to tolerate teachers who continue to fail to nurture creativity in their pupils? How can pupils learn the joys of learning from teachers who have in many cases become abusers of the very children entrusted to them? What has become of the pride of the police uniform with officers looking the part and fit for service? How have we come to the current disturbing trend of overweight officers with their uniforms literally bursting at the seams? How can they catch criminals when they look so unfit?

Fourth, the private sector as the engine of growth and wealth creation plays an important role as corporate citizen in our young democracy. There are sadly still too many in this sector asking what the state can do for them, rather than what they can do to contribute to a more prosperous society with greater equity. The performance of the state as an enabler of a better business environment has been admirable.

Critics of GEAR are disingenuous in not acknowledging that, given the realities of the competitive global knowledge economy we operate in, this was the best economic policy choice we could make. All over the world, governments have come to accept the importance of positioning their economies for the competitive climate wrought by globalisation. Social democrats, new labour, new democrats, even communist China are all rising to this challenge. What we need is to improve our ability to implement socio-economic policies in a more coherent manner to reap the full benefits of our macro-economic stability.

It is also fair to say that a significant proportion of the private sector still operates on an extractive industry model that focuses on excess profits with little attention to sustainability. Too much emphasis is placed on compliance rather than expanding the bounds of possibility offered by the new legislative framework. For example, black economic empowerment framed as an opportunity to enhance economic participation and thus grow the economic cake generates exciting possibilities in which everyone wins: traditional white business, new entrants, higher quality customer service and greater corporate social investment. A compliance approach that characterises a significant proportion of the deals concluded to date has made lawyers and the financial sector the greatest winners thus far.

The same can be said for the grudging implementation of employment equity. If we had all co-invested in the development of high-level skills over the past eleven years, we would have broken the back of the legacy of skills shortages by now. But many in the private sector still believe that they can get away with a minimalist investment approach and depend on poaching skills from competitors. This is short-sighted.

Finally, the media could play an even greater role by exploiting the freedom of the press we now enjoy, to enhance its performance. Many are already doing a great job. But there is significant under-performance in the quality of news coverage in many sectors of the print, audio and visual media. The watchdog, investigative and educational roles of the media need further impetus as part of the media's stewardship. Much higher investments are needed in training to enhance the skills of the many young professionals who are eager, but inexperienced. No democracy can function adequately without a robust free press. The media must rise to the occasion.

SUGGESTED WAY FORWARD

There are a number of factors that have constrained the emergence of stewardship amongst citizens. The authoritarian nature of past regimes promoted a passive citizenry. The post-apartheid state compounded this passive culture by positioning itself as a developmental state ready to intervene in the critical areas of society in order to shape the pace and form of the transformation process. Post-apartheid rhetoric, including the ANC's 1994 election platform that promised houses, water, education, etc., also created a culture of dependence on the government to fix everything. The anxiety to signal a break from an uncaring state to a people's government had the unintended consequence of demobilising the civil society activism that was the hallmark of the 1980s and 1990s. Those who have been waiting for eleven years for the "promised land" are beginning to show signs of passive aggression. Expressions of anger take forms that further indicate a disconnection with ownership of public resources. Trashing and burning assets is not compatible with stewardship.

I would like to suggest a few pointers to give greater practical effect to our stewardship as citizens of this beloved country.

First, we have to constantly put the vision of our democracy in front of us as we go about our daily chores. Our vision is of a free democratic non-racial, non-sexist and more equitable society. Let us remember Harding's words: "... where there is no vision, we lose the sense of our great power to transcend history and create a new future for ourselves with others, and we perish utterly in hopelessness, mutual terror and despair. Therefore, this quest (for a vision) is not a luxury; life itself demands it of us".⁶

Second, let us recommit to the values that are enshrined in our Constitution. They give meaning to who we are as a nation and provide a basis for social stability. A French writer, Jacques Monod, had this to say at a symposium of Nobel Laureates in 1969: "No society can survive without a moral code based on values understood, accepted and respected by the majority of its members".⁷ We pride ourselves as South Africans as being inspired by the values embedded in our rights-based Constitution. We have to measure our daily conduct by how well we are doing to live out these values.

Third, in honouring the martyrs of hope today, let us rededicate ourselves to stewardship of the freedom they died fighting for, that affords us the privilege to be who we are today. That requires a leadership style that reflects Sekou Toure's words, which served as an inspiration for Steve Biko: "'In order to achieve real action you must yourself be a living part of Africa and of her thought; you must be an element of the popular energy which is entirely called forth for the freeing, the progress and the happiness of Africa. There is no place outside of that fight for the artist or for the intellectual who is not himself concerned with, or completely at one with, the people in the great battle of Africa and of suffering humanity'".⁸

It is in this spirit that Steve Biko's sons and I would like to announce the establishment of the Stephen Bantu Biko Leadership Fellowship Programme, as part of UCT's 175 Chancellor's Campaign. This postgraduate leadership fellowship programme will serve to further cement the great partnership between UCT and the Steve Biko Foundation. Our company, Circle Capital Ventures, will contribute R5 million, whilst we as UCT alumni will complement this contribution through personal donations over a three-year period to endow this programme. Samora Biko will work with UCT to elaborate on the structure and *modus operandi* of this leadership fellowship programme to promote the development of leadership that encapsulates the values Steve lived and died for.

I hope that each one of you will rise from this occasion determined to rededicate yourselves to renewed stewardship signified in whatever manner you choose. History demands nothing less from us.

Notes

1 Steve Biko. 2004 [1978]. *I Write What I Like*. Johannesburg: Picador Africa, p. 108.
2 Polingaysi Qoyawayma. 1964. In Polingaysi Qoyawayma, Vada Carlson and Elizabeth White. 1977. *No Turning Back: A Hopi Indian Woman's Struggle to Live in Two Worlds*. Albuquerque: University of New Mexico Press, p. 171.
3 Preamble to the Constitution of the Republic of South Africa, 1996 Act No. 108. See www.info.gov.za/documents/constitution/1996/96preamble.htm (accessed 11 June 2009).
4 Aaron Sorkin. 1995. *The American President*. Motion picture directed by Rob Reiner. Beverly Hills: Castle Rock Entertainment.
5 William Nicholson. 1995. *First Night*. Motion picture directed by Arthur Wooster and Jerry Zucker. Culver City: Colombia Pictures.
6 Vincent Harding. 1983. *There is a River: The Black Struggle for Freedom in America*. New York: Random House, p. xii.
7 Jacques Monod. 10 September 1969. Address at the Symposium of Nobel Laureates. Sweden.
8 Sekou Toure. In Steve Biko. 1988 [1978]. *I Write What I Like*. Harmondsworth: Penguin, p. 46.

7

South Africa: A Scintillating Success Waiting to Happen

Speaker: Archbishop Emeritus Desmond Tutu
Date: 26 September 2006

"It is amazing to think that Steve did not have much time to propagate his teachings and in a way, by rights, should have disappeared into oblivion ... He didn't have a flashy car or a big house. He lived in a ghetto township. He did not even have a university degree and by rights, should have been consigned to the oblivion reserved for all non-entities. But what is the reality?"

– Desmond Tutu

South Africa: A Scintillating Success Waiting to Happen

Thank you for the great honour you have bestowed on me by inviting me to give this year's memorial lecture. They tortured and beat Steve up in jail and heartlessly killed him. You will recall that he was driven, comatose, from Port Elizabeth, naked in the back of a Land Rover all the way to Pretoria, where he was shackled to a grate and left to expire, sitting in his urine. He was left to die a death that Mr Jimmy Kruger later said had left him cold. Phew! They had hoped that would be the end, the inglorious, shameful end of someone they considered a pretty handful. They hoped he would be snuffed out like you blow out a candle. Annihilated, and that would be that. But they were doomed to fail.

It is amazing to think that Steve did not have much time to propagate his teachings and in a way, by rights, should have disappeared into oblivion. Yet, this does happen, despite all appearances to the contrary, to be in fact a moral universe. Right, good, justice will ultimately prevail and in this universe, extraordinary greatness is measured by how much the person has served others, how much altruism they have shown, and not by how much they have come to own materially, how much self-aggrandisement has happened.

He didn't have a flashy car or a big house. He lived in a ghetto township. He did not even have a university degree and by rights, should have been consigned to the oblivion reserved for all non-entities. But what is the reality? I was privileged to preach at his mammoth funeral attended by diplomats and people from all corners of South Africa. My wife Leah and several of her friends tried to come from Soweto and were assaulted by the police and prevented from coming. Perhaps it was just as well. King William's Town would have found it difficult to host so many mourners. That was a funeral for a national hero, not a non-entity. There is a statue erected in his honour in East London, unveiled by

Madiba; there was the *Cry Freedom* film; and now this series of lectures at this great university. These are not things you do for a non-entity.

And what about those who tortured and killed him, and those doctors who colluded with them? They have been consigned to the scrap heap of history, mere flotsam and jetsam. Right and goodness have triumphed, even if we still do not have the whole, the true story of how Steve died.

What is more, we have here an eloquent example that true greatness lies in having given oneself on behalf of others. Jesus said: "Greater love hath no one than that a person should lay down his life for others." And the people have said a resounding "Amen" to that, and you really can't fool all of the people all the time. They will always know who their leaders are and they will be ready to acknowledge them and, to the extent that they can, will reward them and express their appreciation to them. You cannot buy that affirmation by the people. We know it – the apartheid regime tried to foist its candidates on us as our leaders, and the people, that is, the vast majority, rejected them as but pseudo leaders. Once people have taken you to their hearts as a true, genuine leader, then nothing anyone tries to do can dislodge the real leader from the hearts of the people.

Steve was a remarkable young man in his commitment and passion. He was willing to abandon his medical studies when he was expelled from medical school; he was ready to jettison it all because of his all-consuming passion to strive for the liberation of his people and their emancipation through appropriate community-development and health-enhancing projects.

He possessed an incisive and indeed massive intellect. Yes, a charismatic individual who made a unique assessment of why black people were always at the end of the queue, at the bottom of the pile. It was a daringly novel diagnosis, that we were collaborators in our own oppression and subjugation, and so he provided the genesis for the Black Consciousness Movement. It really went to the heart of the matter.

Language is not merely innocuous, merely descriptive. No, it has the potency to create the reality that it describes, and being designated "non-European", "non-white" was not merely degrading and humiliating; horrendously it had the power of making a child of God doubt that she was indeed a child of God. That is the blasphemous aspect of oppression and injustice. It did not take long after one had been called non-this, non-the-other, for one to take on the identity of a non-entity, to have this demon of self-hate, self-doubt, of a negative self-image gnawing away at one's being. Now that sounds melodramatic, but let me tell you a story.

In 1972, I was Associate Director of the Theological Education Fund (TEF) of the World Council of Churches based not in Geneva but in London. I had to travel extensively, mainly in sub-Saharan Africa. On my first visit to Nigeria, I had to fly from Lagos to Jos in the north. I boarded the plane and the entire crew was black. Both the captain and the first officer were Nigerian and my heart leapt. I grew inches with pride at this realisation that they contradicted all that apartheid South Africa asserted about blacks. We took off smoothly but some time later hit turbulence. Wow! It was scary. You know, one moment you are up there and then, bump, the aeroplane descends and you leave your stomach on the ceiling. To this day, I am shocked at what happened next. I really did not know the power of conditioning. I got quite scared because I said to myself: "Hey, there's no white man in the cockpit. Will these blacks be able to land us safely?" Can you believe it?

That is what Steve diagnosed in us as our illness, and Black Consciousness was meant to exorcise this demon, to make us realise that, as he said, we were human and not inferior, just as the white person was human and not superior. I internalised what others had decided was to be my identity, not my God-given utterly precious and unique me.

And when I looked inside me and saw this man-made caricature, I bridled with anger and hatred and contempt of this false self. I then projected it outwards to those who outwardly looked like me. Before my superior white overlords I quaked with demeaning obsequiousness, and before those who looked like the thing I hated and despised I was harsh and abrasive.

We used to laugh as we heard the story of the man who answered the telephone and when he heard his white boss's voice, would hurriedly pull off his cap. And yet this same person would be harsh as he excoriated his fellow blacks. You know how the black mine clerks treated the black mine workers, screaming at them to the delight of their white bosses? You recall the brutality of black constables to their own in order to curry favour with their white superiors? Or how someone perhaps to whom you had given a tip would say, thinking they were praising you: "Oh, you're my white boss, *ungu umlungu wam, o lekhoa laka*" or how black domestic workers would declare proudly that they did not work for black employers – this even if they would be paid more. Frequently, of course, they were right because there were no greater exploiters of blacks than their fellow blacks. Or you would see how abominably badly we would often drive in black townships because, fundamentally, we do not respect one another. We used to do things we would never dream of doing in town, like stopping at an awkward point at a street corner – oh, and our taxi drivers, they have taken the cake.

Well, why do I use the past tense? The fact of the matter is that we still, depressingly, do not respect one another. I have often said Black Consciousness did not finish the work it set out to do.

Why have we lost our deeply African reverence for life? Just look at what happens with, say, a car hijacking. The scared owner hands over the keys and for no earthly reason he/she will be shot dead in cold blood for the sheer hell of it, utterly gratuitously, wantonly.

Is it not horrendous to an African, even before Black Consciousness came on the scene, for whatever reason for an adult man to rape a nine-month-old baby? What has come over us? Perhaps we do not realise just how apartheid has damaged us so that we seem to have lost our sense of right and wrong, so that when we go on strike, as is our right to do, we are not appalled that some of us can chuck people out of moving trains because they did not join the strike, or why is it common practice now to trash, to go on the rampage? Striking municipal workers empty trash on the streets, other strikers break shop windows, loot and trash premises. Even our students on strike will often destroy the very facilities they need for their studies. What has happened to us? It seems as if we have perverted our freedom, our rights into licence, into being irresponsible. Rights go hand-in-hand with responsibility, with dignity, with respect for oneself and for the other.

Can you tell me why we think it is okay to litter? Many of us will chuck a banana/orange peel, a paper wrapping on the ground next to a dustbin. Why? Why are we so unmindful of our environment? Of course, many of us still live in poverty and squalor. But you know how, although we were poor long ago, we used to be proud of our surroundings, sweeping even the street. There are many neighbourhoods that make you proud, where people have cultivated lawns and planted gardens and it is all so beautiful, and people who don't care are the first to want to sit on those lawns and they will often litter and leave their trash behind. We must tell those who do this that littering is not only a crime, it is also a sin. We despoil God's creation, of which we are supposed to be stewards, caring for it on behalf of God.

There should be things we consider "infra dig", below our dignity to do. Most, no all, of us here, would not even consider picking up an apple that we were eating if it fell into a dustbin. It should be so with all the bad things we are tolerating, people urinating in public places, etc. There are shops and offices which it is a pleasure to enter. The shop assistants are courteous, friendly, smiling and eager to help, but there are others where they think they are doing you a favour. There are municipal, provincial, government offices which you go to only because you really can't help it. They behave as those others used to behave in the old pass offices – they are rude, inefficient and thoroughly unpleasant. Why, oh why, when it is just as easy to be efficient, friendly and courteous? It is because we don't respect one another, and we don't because we don't respect ourselves first. We despise ourselves, we hate ourselves and we project it on to others.

During our struggle against apartheid we refused to obey unjust laws because, rightly, we wanted to make South Africa ungovernable. We have achieved our goal. We are free. South Africa is a democracy. We have an obligation to obey the laws made by our own legislators. We should be dignified, law-abiding citizens, proud of our beautiful land, proud of our freedom won at such great cost. We should not devalue it. We should not abuse our children, our womenfolk.

We are generous, compassionate, caring people at our best. We give the highest praise when we say, "*Yu, unobuntu, ona lebotho*"; this is someone who cares about others, who is generous and hospitable, who respects others, as she hopes and expects they will respect her.

Hey, we have a wonderful country. We have produced outstanding people. The best memorial to Steve Biko would be a South Africa where everyone respects themselves, has a positive self-image filled with a proper self-esteem, and holds others in high regard.

Hey, we are wonderful people. We have given the world a splendid example in our relatively peaceful transition, showing that former enemies can at least be colleagues. We have shown Northern Ireland, the Middle East, Rwanda, Burma, Sri Lanka, Zimbabwe, the Democratic Republic of the Congo that you can have had a violent past and a peaceful present and future. We have given the world the most admired statesman in Madiba; we have produced a Steve Biko too – the world has marvelled at our capacity to forgive, to walk the path of forgiveness and reconciliation, to be magnanimous and generous.

We must take seriously the cry of those who say, in the past we were not white enough, today we are not black enough, even if they are wrong. We must take seriously their perception to try to change it. We must beware the dangers of ethnic strife. See what it has done in Rwanda, Burundi, Bosnia, Kenya, the Democratic Republic of Congo (DRC). So let us hear the cry of those who complain about a Nguni-ocracy and even of a Xhosa-ocracy. Many a truth is uttered in jest. Let us oppose xenophobia, we who were welcomed by countries that were ready to run the gauntlet of the wrath of the South African Defence Force and let us be magnanimous in victory; let us act sensitively in the matter of name-changing and not appear to gloat and to ride roughshod over the feelings of others. Let us build up a groundswell of consensus to support any name-change and not leave many filled with impotent resentment. Let us try to use name-changes as opportunities for nation building.

For you know what? We are indeed a scintillating success waiting to happen.

8

30th Commemoration of Steve Biko's Death

Speaker: Former President Thabo Mbeki
Date: 12 September 2007

"Steve Biko understood that to attain our freedom we had to rebel against the notion that we are a problem, that we should no longer merely cry out: Why did God make me an outcast and a stranger in mine own house?; that we should stop looking at ourselves through the eyes of others, and measuring our souls by the tape of a world that looks on in amused contempt and pity."

– *Thabo Mbeki*

30th Commemoration of Steve Biko's Death

Director of Ceremonies, members of the Biko family, distinguished guests, ladies and gentlemen: We meet here today to commemorate the death of an outstanding young South African patriot, Stephen Bantu Biko.

The bloody decade of the 1970s in our country, which included the Soweto Uprising of 1976, took the lives of many fighters for our liberation, both young and old. I stand here this evening to speak in celebration of one of the martyrs of this period, Stephen Bantu Biko.

The distinguished and learned audience in this auditorium and the thousands in our country and continent who are listening to this lecture, which is being carried live by our public broadcaster, the SABC, will know that I would have asked myself the question: what should I say on this historic occasion?

Echoing the views of the Nineteenth-century US poet, Walt Whitman, expressed in his poem: "Song of Myself" I too would like to say: "I wish I could translate the hints about the dead young men and women,/And the hints about old men and mothers, and the offspring taken/soon out of their laps./What do you think has become of the young and old men?/And what do you think has become of the women and children?"[1] Perhaps, today, I have no choice but to translate, in the context of our current realities, the hints about our dead young men and women of the 1970s and the following decades, such as Steve Biko, and the hints about old men and mothers, and the offspring, including Steve Biko, taken soon out of their laps.

We have gathered here exactly thirty years to the day after Steve Bantu Biko was murdered by those responsible for the apartheid crime against humanity. We have convened here not to mourn his death, but to celebrate his life, his thoughts and the immense contribution he made to the liberation of our country and people.

I would like sincerely to thank his wife and my sister, Sis' Ntsiki, his son Nkosinathi, the rest of the Biko family, the Biko Foundation, and all who were his close friends and comrades, for the honour they have given me to deliver this particular Biko Memorial Lecture, exactly thirty years after the dark forces of evil cruelly robbed our country, our continent and the world of an outstanding young revolutionary who would, today, have been one of the eminent architects of the new world we are striving to build.

In what now seems to be a long time ago, during the years of our exile, I had the rare privilege to reflect on who Steve Biko was, what his ideas were, what he fought for, how and with whom he strived to realise his ideals, what impact he had on his comrades, our country and people, and what his cruel and untimely death meant to those who had recognised him as a harbinger of a future that, distant as it might have seemed, was nevertheless certain to become tomorrow's happy reality.

The unique opportunity for all this was provided by the visit to Lusaka, Zambia, by an eminent English worker in the creative arts, a militant opponent of oppression wherever it might occur, a passionately loyal friend of our people, a good man – Sir Richard Attenborough. He came into our midst to discuss with the ANC, especially those who knew or had engaged in struggle with and under the leadership of Steve Biko, the script he used to construct the film, *Cry Freedom*.

He came to Lusaka from London because he was determined that the remarkable Steve Biko story should be told to the whole world, and told truthfully. He was convinced that the telling of the story of Steve Biko, which would become known to millions of cinema-goers across the globe, would mobilise these millions to stand up to fight the apartheid crime against humanity that had killed Steve Biko. He came also to tell us the unadorned truth that all feature films of the day could not be produced and successfully marketed without access to the necessary finance, all of which would be provided by people who, regardless of their good souls, nevertheless had to demand that the films they financed would earn the necessary return on the money they had invested.

In the end, regardless of what we thought and said as we interacted with Dick Attenborough, and the impact of all this on the film script, we conceded the right to the film-maker to produce and direct the film that ultimately appeared on cinema screens across the world as *Cry Freedom*, whatever its limitations in terms of a comprehensive representation of who and what Steve Biko was, and what he died for.

During this particular week of intense discussion, I learnt many things about Steve Biko, his life and times, and thoughts and actions, sitting, as it were, at the feet of younger comrades who, inspired by his message and example, had joined the ANC in exile to fulfil the mission for which he had perished in the most painful circumstances.

Born in 1946, Steve Biko was sixteen years old when I left our country to go into exile in 1962. A year earlier, in 1961, when we organised for and launched the African Students Association (ASA), the historical parent, with the African Students Union of South Africa (ASUSA), of the South African Students Association (SASO), I did not meet him.

However, my political history from my early youth at school, and since then, has, to some extent, overlapped with the political life of a close friend and comrade of Steve Biko, Nyameko Barney Pityana.

Barney and I were students and members of the ANC Youth League at Lovedale Institution during the latter years of my studies at this once-renowned centre of learning at Alice, across the Thyume River that separates Lovedale from the neighbouring Fort Hare. I mention this today because the young Barney Pityana served as a vital link between the accumulated national experience and wisdom of the struggle for liberation concentrated in the ANC until it was banned in 1960, and the time in 1969, when he and Steve Biko established SASO, the first organised formation of the Black Consciousness Movement, nine years after the long-established ANC and the very young Pan Africanist Congress (PAC) were banned.

I am very pleased that today, thirty years after the death of his comrade, Barney Pityana is also delivering a lecture on Steve Bantu Biko, far to our north, at the University of South Africa (UNISA) campus in Pretoria/Tshwane. It must surely be something of note that members of the ANC Youth League of fifty years ago speak on the same day, in different geographical settings in our country, to pay tribute to a young patriot who assumed the mantle of leadership during some of the most difficult years of our struggle for liberation, and perished as a result.

In his great epic work, "Emperor Shaka the Great", the late Mazisi Kunene says:

> Those who feast on the grounds of others
> Often are forced into gestures of friendship they do not desire.
> But we are the generation that cannot be bypassed.
> We shall not be blinded by gifts from feasts.
> With our own fire we shall stand above the mountains, as the sun.[2]

These words, which could easily have been uttered by the militant generation of the 1970s to which Steve Biko belonged, are attributed to Shaka, an equally young militant of some one and a half centuries before the turbulences that defined the 1970s. Faced with the resistance of his superiors to the far-reaching military changes that he wanted to introduce, Shaka argued that if the status quo remained, they would not be able to withstand the military assaults of their enemies and thus his people would continue to feast on the grounds of others and accordingly be forced into gestures of friendship they did not desire.

Today, we mark the 30th anniversary of the death of an African patriot who, at a particular time, lit our road to freedom like a burning meteor, shining brighter than the system that had sought to minimise his humanity, along with that of the people whose yearnings he symbolised. To celebrate the life of Stephen Bantu Biko is to invoke a vision that has, over the years, inspired all freedom-loving South

Africans decisively to defeat the monster of apartheid and racism and realise the dream of liberation.

As it must, our commemoration of the death of Steve Biko resonates with heroism, a steely human resolve and a remarkable vision for human freedom, the antithesis of the intolerable racism in our country which the whole world came to characterise as a crime against humanity.

In this regard, we may be forgiven for being so bold as to suggest that, in remembering this brave patriot, we could use this occasion as a metaphor for all that is bitter and all that is sweet in South African history. We are surely entitled to feel bitter at the needless snuffing out of the pulsating life of a freedom fighter by small-minded human beings who had arrogated to themselves the absolute right to determine, with impunity, who should qualify to be considered and treated as a human being.

On the other hand, our souls are surely sweetened by the certain knowledge that the high principles of freedom and equality for which Biko struggled and died have, over time, and because of the determination of our people relentlessly to sustain the struggle for freedom, given birth to the reality of today's free and democratic South Africa.

Like Shaka and many others that came before him, Steve Biko understood very well that "Those who feast on the grounds of others/ Often are forced into gestures of friendship they do not desire".[3]

Biko himself said: "What Black Consciousness seeks to do is to produce at the output end of the process, real black people who do not regard themselves as appendages to white society. This truth cannot be reversed. We do not need to apologise for this because it is true that the white systems have produced throughout the world a number of people who are not aware that they too are people."[4]

It would seem to me that three particular historical circumstances were central to the formation of Steve Biko as an outstanding leader of our revolutionary struggle and an eminent representative of his generation.

The first of these is that Steve Biko's life was defined by the apartheid reality of "separate development", which the National Party sought to create from the first day of its electoral victory in 1948.

The second is that as Steve Biko came into his maturity, the national liberation struggle was in full retreat, arising from the banning of the ANC and the PAC, the destruction of the organised structures of the liberation movement, and the systematic decapitation of the movement by the arrest of its leaders and activists.

The third is that this period of extreme reaction following the Sharpeville Massacre, intended to perpetuate the apartheid system into which Steve Biko was born, seemed totally to have demobilised the oppressed through fear of arrest, torture, imprisonment and death at the hands of the repressive security organs of the apartheid state.

With regard to the first of these historical circumstances, Steve Biko said: "Born shortly before 1948, I have lived all my conscious life in the framework of institutionalised separate development. My friendships, my love, my education, my thinking and every other facet of my life have been carved and shaped within the context of separate development. In stages during my life I have managed to outgrow some of the things the system taught me."[5]

Relating to the second of these circumstances, Steve Biko wrote: "... since the banning and harassment of black political parties a dangerous vacuum has been created. The African National Congress and later the Pan Africanist Congress were banned in 1960 ... ever since, there has been no coordinated opinion emanating from the black ranks. Perhaps the Kliptown (Freedom) Charter – objectionable as the circumstances surrounding it might have been – was the last attempt ever made to instil some amount of positiveness in stating categorically what blacks felt on political questions in the land of their forefathers. After the banning of the black political parties in South Africa, people's hearts were gripped by some kind of foreboding fear for anything political. Not only were politics a closed book, but at every corner one was greeted by a slave-like apathy that often bordered on timidity."⁶

With regard to the third of the historical circumstances to which we have referred, Steve Biko wrote: "Black people under the Smuts government were oppressed but they were still men. They failed to change the system for many reasons which we shall not consider here. But the type of black man we have today has lost his manhood. Reduced to an obliging shell, he looks with awe at the white power structure and accepts what he regards as the 'inevitable position' ... All in all, the black man has become a shell, a shadow of man, completely defeated, drowning in his own misery, a slave, an ox bearing the yoke of oppression with sheepish timidity."⁷

A critically important part of the strategic brilliance of the intervention that Steve Biko and his comrades in the Black Consciousness Movement made to re-energise our liberation struggle was to mobilise the black oppressed around one message that would respond to these three historical circumstances. In a manner of speaking, this meant that the BCM threw one stone to kill three birds! But what was this stone, this particular weapon of struggle?

Authentic and honest African scholarship has consistently recognised the integrity and interconnectedness of the African experience through many centuries, including the experience of the Africans of the Diaspora. One of us among the latter, whom we will always salute as one of our own leaders, was the immortal African-American giant, WEB du Bois. More than a century ago, in 1903, du Bois' groundbreaking treatise, *The Souls of Black Folk*, was published in the United States.

Among other things relevant to what we have to say this evening, du Bois wrote:

> Between me and the other world there is ever an unasked question: unasked by some through feelings of delicacy; by others through the difficulty of rightly framing it. All, nevertheless, flutter round it. They approach me in a half-

hesitant sort of way, eye me curiously or compassionately, and then, instead of saying directly, How does it feel to be a problem? ... I answer seldom a word ....[8]

du Bois then told a story of how white children had suddenly excluded him while they we playing together. He wrote:

> Then it dawned upon me with a certain suddenness that I was different from the others; or like, mayhap, in heart and life and longing, but shut out from their world by a vast veil ...
>
> With other black boys the strife was not so fiercely sunny: their youth shrunk into tasteless sycophancy, or into silent hatred of the pale world about them and mocking distrust of everything white; or wasted itself in a bitter cry: 'Why did God make me an outcast and a stranger in mine own house?' The shades of the prison-house closed round about us all: walls straight and stubborn to the whitest, but relentlessly narrow, tall and unscalable to sons of night who must plod darkly on in resignation, or beat unavailing palms against the stone, or steadily, half hopelessly, watch the streak of blue above.
>
> After the Egyptian and Indian, the Greek and Roman, the Teuton and Mongolian, the Negro is a sort of seventh son, born with a veil, and gifted with second-sight in this American world – a world which yields him no true self-consciousness, but only lets him see himself through the revelation of the other world. It is a peculiar sensation, this double-consciousness, this sense of always looking at one's self through the eyes of others, of measuring one's soul by the tape of a world that looks on in amused contempt and pity.[9]

Steve Biko understood that to attain our freedom we had to rebel against the notion that we are a problem, that we should no longer merely cry out: "Why did God make me an outcast and a stranger in mine own house?"; that we should stop looking at ourselves through the eyes of others, and measuring our souls by the tape of a world that looks on in amused contempt and pity.

He understood that to defeat the brutal racial oppression of the apartheid system, we had to rise up against the very ideology of racism, to internalise in our hearts and minds as the critical driving force inspiring the risen masses, a complete and thorough-going repudiation of all racist ideas and all their consequences.

In this regard, Steve Biko wrote: "The philosophy of Black Consciousness ... expresses group pride and the determination by the blacks to rise and attain the envisaged self. At the heart of this kind of thinking is the realisation by the blacks that the most potent weapon in the hands of the oppressor is the mind of the oppressed. Once the latter has been so effectively manipulated and controlled by the oppressor as to make the oppressed believe that he is a liability to the white man, then there will be nothing the oppressed can do that will really scare the powerful masters. Hence, thinking along lines of Black Consciousness makes the black man see himself as being entire in himself, and not as an extension of a broom or additional leverage to some machine. At the end of it all, he cannot tolerate attempts by anybody to dwarf the significance of his manhood. Once this happens, we shall know that the real man in the black person is beginning to shine through ... Various black groups ... are beginning to rid their minds of imprisoning notions which are the legacy of the control of their attitude by whites".[10]

It was to this that I referred when I said: "A critically important part of the strategic brilliance of the intervention that Steve Biko and his comrades in the Black Consciousness Movement made to re-energise our liberation struggle was to mobilise the black oppressed around one message that would respond to the three historical circumstances that conditioned Steve Biko's development. In a manner of speaking, this meant that the BCM threw one stone to kill three birds! This one stone was the militant and uncompromising offensive to defeat what Steve Biko described as "the most potent weapon in the hands of the oppressor, (the) the mind of the oppressed."[11]

This strategic intervention recognised that to defeat the pernicious apartheid system that held the country in thrall, to rebuild the national liberation movement, to defeat the pervasive atmosphere gripping the country, and therefore to resume the offensive for the overthrow of the apartheid regime, the black masses of our country had to refuse to feast on the grounds of others, often forced into gestures of friendship they did not desire. The historic struggle waged by the Black Consciousness Movement against the inhuman ideology of racism put the spotlight on the fact that the racism upheld by the captains of apartheid was, in fact, but the most pernicious expression of white anti-black racism that emerged in Europe, especially in the Eighteenth-century.

In his 2007 book, *Race and the Construction of the Dispensable Other,* Professor Ben Magubane quotes the Eighteenth-century Scottish Enlightenment philosopher, David Hume, thus: "I am apt to suspect the negroes and in general all other species of men ... to be naturally inferior to whites. There never was a civilised nation of any other complexion than white, nor even any individual eminent either in action or speculation. No ingenious manufactures among them, no arts, no sciences ... Such a uniform and constant difference could not happen in so many countries and ages, if nature had not made an original distinction betwixt these breeds of men."[12]

Professor Magubane also quotes one Edward Long, an admirer of David Hume, who wrote *The History of Jamaica,* published in 1774. In this book, Long describes Africans as " 'proud, lazy, treacherous, thievish, hot and addicted to all kinds of lust, and most ready to promote them in others, as pimps, panders, incestuous, brutish and savage, cruel and revengeful, devourers of human flesh, and quaffers of human blood, inconstant, base, treacherous and cowardly; fond of and addicted to all sorts of superstition and witchcraft; and, in a word, to every vice that came in their way, or within their reach ... They are inhuman, drunkards, deceitful, covetous and perfidious to the highest degree ... It is as impossible to be an African and not lascivious, as it is impossible to be born in Africa and not be an African ... (Their) faculties are truly bestial, no less their commerce with other sexes; in these acts they are libidinous and shameless as monkeys, or baboons. The equally hot temperament of their women has given probability to the charge of their admitting these animals frequently to their embrace.'"[13]

To come closer home, Professor Magubane quotes Cecil Rhodes, then Premier of the Cape Colony, as having said: "'I will lay down my own policy on this Native Question. Either you receive them on an equal footing as citizens, or call them a subject race. Well, I have made up my mind ... that we have to treat the natives, where they are in a state of barbarism, in a different way from ourselves. We are to be lords over them ... The native is to be treated as a child and denied the franchise.'"[14]

Contributing his share to the deluge of demeaning racist insults, General Smuts said: "'Natives have the simplest minds, understand only simple ideas or ideals, and are almost animal-like in the simplicity of their minds and ways ... They are different not only in colour but in minds and in political capacity, and their political institutions should be different, while always proceeding on the basis of self-government'".[15]

When Steve Biko said: "What Black Consciousness seeks to do is to produce at the output end of the process real black people who do not regard themselves as appendages to white society",[16] he signalled a revolutionary uprising against more than two centuries of a racist ideology that had been used to justify slavery, imperialism, colonialism and apartheid.

He argued that the black people had to reassert their self-worth, their confidence in themselves as makers of history, reclaim their human dignity and define themselves, rather than look at themselves through the eyes of others, measuring their souls by the tape of a world that looks on in amused contempt and pity, to use WEB du Bois' words. He argued that these masses had the obligation to undo the damage that had been done by "white systems (that) have produced throughout the world a number of people who are not aware that they too are people".[17]

None of us present here today can question the reality that the Black Consciousness Movement brought into our liberation struggle, during a decade of the greatest general retreat of the liberation movement on many fronts since the ANC was formed in 1912, served as one of the principal catalysts that ended the general retreat. It helped to open the way to the two-decade-long general offensive on all fronts, that triumphed with the victory of the democratic revolution in 1994.

However, the challenge posed by Steve Biko and the Black Consciousness Movement, especially to the black people, did not lose its relevance with our historic victory of 1994.

I speak here of the challenge to defeat the centuries-old attempt "to dwarf the significance of (our) manhood",[18] to treat us as children, to define us as sub-humans whom nature has condemned to be inferior to white people, an animal-like species characterised by limited intellectual capacity, bestiality, lasciviousness and moral depravity, obliged, in our own interest, to accept that the white segment of humanity should, in perpetuity, serve as our lord and master.

As I speak here today, to celebrate the life of an outstanding son of our people, a selfless patriot and fearless revolutionary, Steve Bantu Biko, I must respond to what Walt Whitman commanded, and try with reference to our contemporary reality, thirteen years after the victory of the Democratic Revolution, to "translate the hints about the dead young men and women,/And the hints about old men and mothers, and the offspring/taken soon out of their laps".[19]

Together, including the latter-day admirers of Steve Biko, some of whom seek to redefine him by stripping him of his revolutionary credentials and place him outside the continuum of our more than century-old national democratic struggle and movement, we must critically examine our society today. In this context, we must ask ourselves whether the majority of our people, for whose freedom Steve Biko sacrificed his life, are truly aware that they too are people, and whether they do not, still, regard themselves as appendages of our self-appointed superiors.

Together we must pose the question and answer it honestly – have all of us accepted that nobody should be obliged to feast on the grounds of others? Has the majority taken advantage of its victory in 1994 to repudiate the practice of resorting to forced gestures of friendship it does not desire?

Have we all, the former oppressor and former oppressed national groups, broken down the walls of what WEB du Bois described as a "prison-house", which was constructed to represent and give permanence to the seemingly incontrovertible truth that those who are white had a manifest destiny to govern and civilise those who are black, and those who are black should, in their own interest, accept the white people as their benevolent and caring guardians, however cruel, insulting and inhumane their conduct?

In his work, *The Coloniser's Model of the World,* the historian JM Blaut says: "This belief is the notion that European civilisation – the West – has had some unique historical advantage, some special quality of race or culture or environment or mind or spirit, which gives this human community a permanent superiority over all other communities, at all times in history and down to the present ... Therefore, the world has a permanent geographical centre and a permanent periphery; an Inside and an Outside. Inside leads, Outside lags. Inside innovates, Outside imitates."[20]

Reflecting on this racist and hegemonic Eurocentrism in his 2001 paper, "The Metamorphosis of Colonialism", immanent in the commercial process of globalisation, Jeremy Seabrook writes: "Alien values are implanted into the lives of the people ... alien, not merely in the sense of foreign or exotic, but alien to humanity ... At first it was partly resisted, but with time, it became more and more acceptable, until it has now become a major determinant on the lives of the young, displacing all earlier forms of acculturation, other ways of answering need, other ways of being in the world. This process of forgetting, beyond recall, but perhaps not quiet beyond reclamation, is a form of colonialism far more effective than that which held so much of the world in thrall in an earlier empire."[21]

Caught between the pincers of a mind-set that educated us to imagine and internalise the notion of an Inside that leads, and an Outside that lags, an Inside that innovates, and an Outside that imitates, and objective social reality that dictates that we should forget our identity and historical and human value systems, beyond recall, we must ask ourselves the challenging question – have we liberated ourselves from what Steve Biko identified as the "imprisoning (and demeaning) notions which are the legacy of the control of (our) attitude by whites?"[22]

In this regard, he said: "One writer makes the point that in an effort to destroy completely the structures that had been built up in the African Society and to impose their imperialism with an unnerving totality, the colonialists were not satisfied merely with holding a people in their grip and emptying the Native's brain of all form and content; they turned to the past of the oppressed people and distorted, disfigured and destroyed it. No longer was reference made to African culture; it became barbarism. Africa was 'the dark continent'. Religious practices and customs were referred to as superstition. The history of African Society was reduced to tribal battles and internecine wars ... No wonder the African child learns to hate his heritage in his days at school. So negative is the image presented to him that he tends to finds solace only in close identification with the white society ... No doubt, therefore, part of the approach envisaged in bringing about 'black consciousness' has to be directed to the past, to seek to rewrite the history of the black man and to produce in it the heroes who form the core of the African background ... A people without a positive history is like a vehicle without an engine ... Then too one can extract from our indigenous cultures a lot of positive virtues which could teach the Westerner a lesson or two".[23]

In his well-known book, *Decolonising the Mind*, the Kenyan novelist and writer, Ngugi wa Thiong'o, describes a stormy debate that once took place at the University of Nairobi about the restructuring of the English Department. Ngugi says: "Three African lecturers and researchers at the university responded ... by calling for the abolition of the English Department as then constituted. They questioned the underlying assumption that the English tradition and the emergence of the modern West were the central root of Kenya's and Africa's consciousness and cultural heritage. They rejected the underlying notion that Africa was an extension of the West. Then followed the crucial rejoinder: Here then, is our main question: if there is a need for a study of the historic continuity of a single culture, why can't this be African? Why can't African literature be at the centre so that we can view other cultures in relationship to it?"[24]

This, of course, raises the question – what is African culture? What constitutes an African identity, the opposite of the negative stereotype of ourselves which colonialism and racism presented to the African child so that he or she tended to find solace only in close identification with the white society?

During our years of liberation, many voices have been raised, expressing grave concern at the prevalence of many negative developments in our society. One of these is the incidence of crime and the particular forms some of these crimes assume. These would include the rape of children and women, including the elderly. They would also include murders that suggest the most callous disdain for the value of human life. Similarly, many have expressed concern at what seems to be an entrenched value system centred on the personal acquisition of wealth at all costs and by all means, including wilful resort to corruption and fraud.

These negative social phenomena and others, which occasioned the call for moral regeneration, have suggested that our society has been captured by a rapacious individualism which is corroding our social cohesion, which is repudiating the value and practice of human solidarity, and which totally rejects the fundamental precept of *ubuntu–umntu ngumntu ngabanye*.

The question is therefore posed correctly – is this the kind of society that Steve Biko visualised, that he fought and died for? When he wrote: "The philosophy of Black Consciousness ... expresses group pride and the determination by the blacks to rise and attain the envisaged self",[25] surely he did not imagine an "envisaged self" characterised by the rapacious and venal individualism we have just mentioned.

To reclaim or rediscover the African identity and build a society that is new not only in its political and economic arrangements, but also in terms of the values it upholds, somewhat tentative calls have been made to re-educate our society about the *ubuntu* value system.

As did the African lecturers and researchers at the University of Nairobi, perhaps we too should ask the question – why can't an African world view, such as *ubuntu*, be at the centre, so that we can view other cultures in relationship to it?

Ubuntu, which reminds us that "a person is a person through other people", does not allow for an individualism that overrides the collective interests of a community.

It stands in contra-distinction to the idea that an individual is the be-all and end-all, without, at the same time, positing that an individual is right-less or dispensable in the grand scheme of things.

Ubuntu places a premium on the values of human solidarity, compassion and human dignity. It is a lived philosophy that enables members of the community to achieve higher results through collective efforts. It is firmly based on recognising the humanity in everyone. It emphasises the importance of knowing oneself and accepting the uniqueness in all of us so as to render meaningless the complexes of inferiority and superiority. Indeed, *ubuntu* connects all of humanity, irrespective of ethnicity or racial origins.

Clearly, the onset of democracy has opened up space for our indigenous cultures to assert themselves as historical agencies in and of themselves, of course influenced by the imperatives thrown up by current socio-political conditions. And yet we must admit that we have so far failed to use these historical agencies to infuse into our society the new value system that must replace the value construct that was an attendant part of the socio-economic reality that emerged during and out of the long years of colonialism and apartheid.

In that sense, we must admit that we have not, as yet, accomplished all the tasks that Steve Biko and his comrades set when they called for an uprising against the ideology of racism which was born in Europe, and the re-assertion of our pride and dignity.

In this regard, Steve Biko wrote: "In rejecting Western values ... we are rejecting those things that are not only foreign to us, but that seek to destroy the most cherished of our beliefs – that the cornerstone of society is man himself – not just his welfare, not his material wellbeing but just man himself with all his ramifications. We reject the power-based society of the Westerner that seems to be ever concerned with perfecting their technological know-how while losing out on their spiritual dimension. We believe that in the long run, the special contribution to the world by Africa will be in this field of human relationships. The great powers of the world may have done wonders in giving the world an industrial and military look, but the great gift still has to come from Africa – giving the world a more human face".[26]

When Steve Biko made this prophecy, saying after Mazisi Kunene: "With our own fire we shall stand above the mountains, as the sun,"[27] he was following in the footsteps of other great giants of our liberation struggle.

In his famous 1906 address, "The Regeneration of Africa", Pixley ka Isaka Seme said: "The regeneration of Africa means that a new and unique civilisation is soon to be added to the world. The African is not a proletarian in the world of science and art. He has precious creations of his own, of ivory, of copper and of gold, fine, plated willow-ware and weapons of superior workmanship. Civilisation resembles an organic being in its development – it is born, it perishes, and it can propagate itself. More particularly, it resembles a plant, it takes root in the teeming earth, and when the seeds fall in other soils new varieties sprout up. The most essential departure of this new civilisation is that it shall be thoroughly spiritual and humanistic – indeed a regeneration moral and eternal!"[28] In his 1961 Nobel Lecture, entitled "Africa and Freedom", Inkosi Albert Luthuli enlarged on this vision and said:

> Still licking the scars of past wrongs perpetrated on her, could (Africa) not be magnanimous and practise no revenge? Her hand of friendship scornfully rejected, her pleas for justice and fair-play spurned, should she not nonetheless seek to turn enmity into amity? Though robbed of her lands, her independence and opportunities – this, oddly enough, often in the name of civilisation and even Christianity – should she not see her destiny as being that of making a distinctive contribution to human progress and human relationships with a peculiar new African flavour enriched by the diversity of cultures she enjoys, thus building on the summits of present human achievement an edifice that would be one of the finest tributes to the genius of man? She should see this hour of her fulfilment as a challenge to her to labour on until she is purged of racial domination, and as an opportunity of reassuring the world that her national aspiration lies, not in overthrowing white domination to replace it by a black caste, but in building a non-racial democracy that shall be a monumental brotherhood, a 'brotherly community' with none discriminated against on grounds of race or colour ...
>
> Africa's qualification for this noble task is incontestable, for her own fight has never been and is not now a fight for conquest of

land, for accumulation of wealth or domination of peoples, but for the recognition and preservation of the rights of man and the establishment of a truly free world for a free people."[29]

The challenging question we must ask ourselves is – have we used the freedom for which Steve Biko sacrificed his life to position our country to contribute to an African civilisation that is "thoroughly spiritual and humanistic – indeed a regeneration moral and eternal"[30], as Pixley Seme said; that will make "a distinctive contribution to human progress and human relationships with a peculiar new African flavour enriched by the diversity of cultures she enjoys, thus building on the summits of present human achievement an edifice that would be one of the finest tributes to the genius of man"[31], as Albert Luthuli said; that will bestow "the great gift (to humanity of) giving the world a more human face"[32]; as Steve Biko said?

We dare not allow this noble vision handed down to us by these great titans of our struggle to perish. Its translation into reality, first of all in our own country, must surely be the monument we build in memory of a dear son of our people, Stephen Bantu Biko.

Steve Biko, like Shaka, belonged to a generation that could not be bypassed. As he died at only thirty-one years old, his life's work had just begun. But he left us with the task to translate into our programmes intended to give birth to a new society, the hints about the dead young men and women of his generation, and the hints about old men and mothers, and the offspring taken soon out of their laps.

Dr Wendy Orr has written in the *Sunday Independent* that in the Steve Biko file kept at the headquarters of the Department of Justice, Steve is reported as having said to his killers: "I ask for water to wash myself with and also soap, a washing cloth and a comb. I want to be allowed to buy food. I live on bread only here. Is it compulsory for me to be naked? I am naked since I came here".[33]

These few and simple words, which speak to the most basic human needs, tell everything that needs to be told about why Steve Biko was right to dedicate his life to the defeat of the criminal ideology of racism, to liberate our country from the clutches of racist fanatics to whom the souls of black folk meant nothing.

When he ceased to breathe, at the cruel and callous hands of his torturers, his was what the poet Ben Okri would describe as "a gigantic death".[34] But, at the same time, this gigantic death of a man deliberately kept by his captors naked and unwashed, also constituted "an enormous birth". And so it is that we must listen carefully to what the poet, Ben Okri, said in his "Mental Flight".

> ... A sense of the limited time we have
> Here on earth to live magnificently
> To be as great and happy as we can
> To explore our potential to the fullest
> And to lose our fear of death
> Having gained a greater love
> And reverence for life
> And its incommensurable golden brevity
> So it is with this moment
> A gigantic death
> And an enormous birth.
> In timelessness.[35]

From the gigantic death of Stephen Bantu Biko thirty years ago today, must, in time, arise an enormous birth. Stephen Bantu Biko died, but his vision has not perished. I thank you for your attention.

Notes

1 Walt Whitman. 1855. *Song of Myself*. Ll.: 31–36. See www.web-books.com/Classics/Poetry/Anthology/Whitman/SongOfMy.htm (accessed 11 June 2009).
2 Mazisi Kunene. 1979. *Emperor Shaka the Great: A Zulu Epic*. Johannesburg: Heinemann Educational Books, p. 55, 1l.: 18–22.

3. Kunene, *Emperor Shaka the Great*, p. 55, ll.: 18–19.
4. Steve Biko. 2004 [1978]. *I Write What I Like*. Johannesburg: Picador Africa, p. 56.
5. Biko, *I Write What I Like*, p. 29.
6. Biko, *I Write What I Like*, p. 37.
7. Biko, *I Write What I Like*, p. 30.
8. William Edward Burghardt du Bois. 1961 [1903]. *The Souls of Black Folk: Essays and Sketches*. Charleston: Forgotten Books, p. 3.
9. Du Bois, *The Souls of Black Folk*.
10. Biko, *I Write What I Like*, p. 74.
11. Biko, *I Write What I Like*, p. 74.
12. Bernard Magubane. 2007. *Race and the Construction of the Dispensable Other*. Pretoria: University of South Africa Press.
13. Magubane, *Race and the Construction of the Dispensable Other*.
14. Magubane, *Race and the Construction of the Dispensable Other*.
15. Magubane, *Race and the Construction of the Dispensable Other*.
16. Biko, *I Write What I Like*, p. 55.
17. William Edward Burghardt du Bois. Unknown source.
18. Biko, *I Write What I Like*, p. 74.
19. Whitman, *Song of Myself*, ll.: 31–34.
20. Jim Blaut. 1993. *The Colonizer's Model of the World: Geographical Diffusionism and Eurocentric History*. New York: The Guilford Press.
21. Jeremy Seabrook. 1995. "The Metamorphosis of Colonialism". In *Dominance of the West over the Rest*. Selangor: Just Word Press.
22. Biko, *I Write What I Like*, p. 74.
23. Biko, *I Write What I Like*, pp. 31–32.
24. Ngugi wa Thiong'o. 1986. *Decolonising the Mind*. Oxford: James Currey, p. 94.
25. Biko, *I Write What I Like*, p. 74.
26. Biko, *I Write What I Like*, p. 51.
27. Kunene, *Emperor Shaka the Great*, l.: 22.
28. Pixley ka Isaka Seme. 1906. "The Regeneration of Africa". Address to the Royal Africa Society. London. See www.blackpast.org/?q=1906-isaka-seme-regeneration-africa (accessed 11 June 2009).
29. Inkosi Albert Luthuli. 10 December 1961. "Africa and Freedom". Acceptance speech on winning the 1960 Nobel Peace Prize. Oslo. See www.jstor.org/pss/4184285 (accessed 11 June 2009).
30. Seme, "The Regeneration of Africa".
31. Luthuli, "Africa and Freedom".
32. Biko, *I Write What I Like*, p. 51.
33. Wendy Orr. *Sunday Independent*.
34. Ben Okri. 1999. *Mental Flight: An Anti-Spell for the 21st Century*. Nairobi.
35. Okri, *Mental Flight*.

9

Energising Democracy: Rights and Responsibilities

Speaker: Former Finance Minister Trevor Manuel
Date: 11 September 2008

"There cannot be any doubt that from the point of the decision to establish a Black Student movement, to every living moment until Steve's last breath on 12 September 1977, and beyond that to the elections of 27 April 1994 and indeed until today, the focus of our passions and energies has been and remains the fundamental transformation of society."

– *Trevor Manuel*

Energising Democracy: Rights and Responsibilities

I cannot sufficiently express the honour bestowed by the invitation to deliver this ninth Steve Biko Memorial Lecture. I want to sincerely thank the members of both the Biko family and the Biko Foundation for the privilege they thus bestow. I also want to express my deep appreciation to each of you for being here; your time and energy are amongst your greatest assets, thank you for giving up some of it to be here.

This lecture takes place at a time when, as a country, we are going through some trying growth pains; together we are searching for inspiration, seeking guidance and yearning for leadership. Our country is undergoing a complex and sometimes painful examination of its foundations, its values and its institutions. It is at times such as this that a nation has to dig deep within itself, take careful observations and focus on repairing its soul.

During such trying times, it is not uncommon for us Africans to seek the wisdom of our departed ancestors, and it is the life's work of Bantu Steve Biko that we today look to for such wisdom.

Biko's writings speak less of his attitude towards the racist governors than it does about the psychology and consciousness of the oppressed. He understood then as we must now, that the consciousness of the poor and their active participation as agents of change in their own lives is the key to democratic transformation. For these beliefs, Biko gave his life in the name of freedom and democracy. For this, we owe him a debt of gratitude and he certainly deserves his rightful place in our collective memories.

There cannot be any doubt that from the point of the decision to establish a Black Student movement, to every living moment until Steve's last breath on 12 September 1977, and beyond that to the elections of 27 April 1994 and indeed until today, the focus of our passions and energies has been and remains the fundamental transformation of society.

The struggle for the humanisation of society and for the full realisation of human rights has always been an important dimension of the broader struggle. With some variation, this was the cornerstone of the policy statements of every organisation ever convened to mobilise for freedom. But, if it were ever merely a struggle for human rights, we could have declared "mission accomplished" in 1994 when we retooled and took over all of the key institutions of government.

In many respects, that moment, at the start of 27 April 1994, when the orange, white and blue flag was lowered for the last time and the flag which has come to symbolise democracy was first hoisted, was for us a less militaristic equivalent of the arrival of the triumphant revolutionary forces marching into the conquered city. In all of the revolutions that so inflamed our passions, the question was what happened after the troops arrived and so for us, the question has to be what happened after we pronounced our own triumphs.

How do we want our successes to be measured? Is it the number of millionaires we create or the opportunities we create for the poor we lift out of poverty? Would it be in the number of black people who now own expensive German sedans, who enjoy seven-digit salaries or occupy estates valued at many millions of rands?

The more appropriate measure is rather to be seen in the profile of poverty that still manifests the same features of race, class and gender that were obtained in December 1968 when "those angry young men walked out of the National Union of South African Students (NUSAS) to establish the South African Students Organisation".

The harsh and ugly truth that confronts us is that forty years after the establishment of SASO and almost fifteen years into democracy, the everyday lives of many of our people remains as uninspired and as filled with despair as it was then. Surely then, a better measure of our collective success is in the numbers of black people who are lifted from poverty, in the measurable interruption of intergenerational poverty and in those instances where we use the power of the state to countervail to take families and communities out of the shadow cast by apartheid's history of denial.

If one were to step outside of this great auditorium and stand on the Jameson steps, one would see both the squalor of many of our townships and informal settlements as well as the stark inequalities that still dominate our cityscapes. The areas where there is a high crime rate are also the areas with the highest TB infection rates. They are also the areas with some of the worst-performing schools. We can see the poverty, pockets of mediocrity, where lives have not changed.

Biko's writing on consciousness reminded me of a quote by Karl Marx on the same matter. "It is not the consciousness of men that determines their being, but, on the contrary, their social being that determines their consciousness."[1] Where the physical environment and poor quality of public services combine to create a sense of abandonment, despair takes root.

Such despair finds an outlet in action against others who appear to be escaping it whether they are peers determined to find a way out, women in the neighbourhood, a family who has a few more earthly possessions or families who speak a different language. What we observe are base instincts that threaten the objectives of freedom and democracy.

It is the absence of consciousness that sees some of the worst excesses of crime and social ills in areas such as Nyanga, Khayelitsha, Mitchells Plain and Manenberg, all almost within the sights of Jameson Hall. We must appreciate that these areas are also home to many of the families who sacrificed greatly to deliver democracy. We must be aware that in all of these areas there are activists who are working hard to roll back this apparent tide of despair. We must pause to consider why this terrible reality exists in the lives of our people.

Perhaps there is something consistently wrong in our communication of the message of freedom, perhaps we have lulled our people into a sense that the struggle had ended at the precise moment when the flag changed. Perhaps it was because we facilitated in the demobilisation of the organs of civil society that had, after all, been the engine of the mass democratic movement and I use the word 'facilitated' because the demobilisation occurred because the individuals who led these organisations were needed as public representatives and public servants.

Or perhaps this happened because those who went into government lost their bearings and replaced everything we understood about social solidarity with a notion of cash transfers, more pensions, and grants.

We ask these questions because this is a moment where we are searching for guidance from ourselves. Perhaps it affords us the time to reflect, to take stock of the unemployed, to understand why we witnessed the appalling violence. And we must understand this, knowing that moments of crises can become moments of opportunity.

As Roberto Unger, a Brazilian philosopher and now a Minister in President Lula's cabinet writes, "the internal dynamics of societies, the revelations of inescapable conflicts and missed opportunities, are the proximate cause of their transformation".[2]

I am sharing this with you speaking as a cabinet minister, as a member of parliament (both of which I have been since 1994), and as member of the national executive committee of the African National Congress. In sharing these examples, I speak of work undone. Some might be of the view that it is wrong for somebody occupying the positions I do to be this candid or to talk so frankly.

Some might even say that I am being reckless since our fourth democratic elections are scheduled in just a few months and opposition parties will feed on this story. I disagree with those views. We must recognise that there are a series of remarkable achievements in South Africa since the dawn of democracy and I can quote figures and examples chapter and verse.

We have made good progress in extending schooling, in broadening access to health care, in extending social security, in providing people with housing, water, sanitation and electricity.

But our quest is for a democracy that must have a palpable presence in the lives of all of our people. Understanding the xenophobic violence that occurred is by no means an attempt to justify it or legitimise it. On the contrary, it is a call to action, a call for a consciousness of what our priorities should be and where we are failing.

The violence that racked our country is a reminder that our struggle is for a transformed society and we need to understand what remains untransformed. Our determination is to serve our people and, I am afraid, that if we don't know our people and we don't know of their lives, then we are probably serving only ourselves and our consciences.

It is to try and understand those gaps that exist between our very best endeavours in government, in the laws we pass, the finances we allocate, the policies we have adopted and the pubic servants we employ, between all of that and the lived reality of our people's lives, that we return to the source of our inspiration today.

Steve Biko wrote: "It is perhaps fitting to start by examining why it is necessary for us to think collectively about a problem we never created. In doing so, I do not wish to concern myself unnecessarily with the white people of South Africa, but to get to the right answers, we must ask the right questions; we have to find out what went wrong where and when, and we have to find out whether our position is a deliberate creation of God or an artificial fabrication of the truth by power-hungry people whose motive is authority, security, wealth and comfort, in other words, the 'Black Consciousness' approach would be irrelevant in a colourless and non-exploitative, egalitarian society. It is relevant here because we believe that an anomalous situation is a deliberate creation of man".[3]

Well, we have confirmed that the country we know, our South Africa, almost fifteen years into democracy remains, despite our best efforts, a country quite far from the "colourless and non-exploitative, egalitarian society"[4] that Biko wrote of. So the issues of consciousness have to be as relevant now as they were then. Freedom must be about conscientisation.

Biko's lesson for the debates in our society speaks of people's consciousness, of their understanding of empowerment. Empowerment, in turn, is about giving people a stake in democracy, in energising democracy. It speaks of a necessary shift from a mere focus on representative democracy to the imperative of an energised democracy.

What constitutes an energised democracy? It surely cannot be the mere occupation of the institutions of democracy (and they are ours in all the arms of government, the legislature, the judiciary and the executive) and the ability to pass laws.

We are, after all, past masters at writing statute; we have passed 1 221 pieces of legislation since 1994. Roberto Unger discusses the concept of a high-energy democracy. He calls for "a set of institutional arrangements that ensure a continuing high level of organised popular engagement in politics". He goes on to say, "a cold, demobilised politics cannot serve as a means to reorganise society. A hot, mobilised politics is compatible with democracy only when institutions channel its energies. It is a goal that can be achieved as the cumulative and combined effect of many devices."[5]

Unger explains what it means to establish a high energy-democracy as – "one that permanently raises the level of organised popular participation in politics, engages the electorate as well as the parties in the rapid and decisive resolution of differences and equips government to rescue people from entrenched and localised situations of disadvantage from which they are unable to exit by the normal forms of political and economic initiative."[6] In drawing inspiration from Unger, there are two elements of an energised democracy that I wish to discuss in some detail today. The first is the role of people and communities in energising democracy. The second relates to a social compact, defining a common understanding of each of the rights and responsibilities of various social formations in energising our democracy, in deepening the gains of our revolution and in improving the lives of all of our people.

Biko's writings sneer at the notion of a passive mass of poor people waiting for a government or a leader to deliver unto them what they seek. He also detested a perspective of development as something that government hands out to people as though it were some type of product or commodity. Under apartheid, it was abundantly clear that development was not a gesture of goodwill conferred by the state. In many respects the starkness of the contradiction between the state and the people focused the mind then.

It would have been antithetical to all that defined us and our notions of freedom to believe, even momentarily, that they came as gestures of goodwill. Instead, development has to begin with a consciousness amongst people that they have power. Now, they have the power to elect their own representatives, to hold them accountable, to build institutions of democracy, to talk to each other to resolve differences, to demand functioning public services.

People must have the consciousness to understand what development means, to understand what empowerment means, for these are not goodies handed out from mountain tops or at the local welfare office.

Professor Zakes Mda, in the 2001 Biko memorial lecture, made the following observation: "Steve Biko and his colleagues did not only take our culture from a protest mode to that of challenge and resistance, they were hands-on activists who established practical community-development projects. These men and women went beyond moaning and whinging about the plight of black people; they made their hands dirty ... building health centres and running them, and facilitating the establishment of communal gardens in marginalised communities. In this way, they aimed to inculcate values of self-reliance and self-development in addition to self-esteem, self-respect and self-confidence".[7]

I am not suggesting that government must abdicate its responsibilities. Government has roles and responsibilities that it must play and play more effectively. What I am calling for is for more people's power, for a deeper understanding of development and for a richer discourse on empowerment.

Let us accept that distorted notions of democracy abound. There are people amongst us, including in government, who want to nurture the notion that empowerment is something that can be dispensed, or worse, that empowerment is exclusively about conferring some right to the rapid accumulation of material wealth.

Frequently this arises for self-serving reasons of power over the lives of others. Government cannot deliver development single-handedly, it can and must partner with active and conscious communities to effect real transformation. Yes, government delivers housing or health care or schooling, but these things only contribute towards development if there is a deeper consciousness about what development is. A patronage-serving culture of delivery and empowerment constitutes a significant threat to our value system and our notion of consciousness.

Let us pause and examine how communities are demobilised. Amongst the first significant pieces of legislation was the 1996 South African Schools Act (Act 84 of 1996) which created, in every school, a governing body. The objective is abundantly clear: parents have a direct and enduring interest in the education of their children and the school should be accountable to a community of parents.

There are 27 000 schools dotted in every community in our country, large or small, institutions that ought to be accountable to the communities they serve.

Yet, this year, the ANC's January 8 statement speaks to "the non-negotiable of education" as being "teachers at school, in class, on time, teaching, no abuse of learners, no neglect of duty".[8] The fact that these matters were included in this otherwise celebratory statement speaks to a real set of problems encountered. With the best will in the world, national government sitting in Tshwane or even a provincial government sitting in the provincial capital is unable to monitor teacher attendance, whether teaching is actually taking place or whether students are in class learning. Without the integral involvement of communities, we don't stand a chance of improving the quality of schooling, especially in poor communities.

Each year when the matric results are issued, the media focus on the schools that have produced excellent results as well as schools where the results leave much to be desired. The Human Science Research Council (HSRC) has a unit whose sole job it is to try to understand what works in driving school performance.

These researchers find poor schools with good results and study them in some detail. In almost all cases where poor schools have done excellent work, there are three factors that stand out. Firstly, they find the presence of a competent and dedicated school principal. Secondly, these schools have teachers who are dedicated, who are prepared and who spend long hours with learners. Thirdly and critically important, these schools have developed solid relationships with parents and the communities within which they are located.

Our legal framework facilitates community involvement in the running of our schools. However, we have not gone far enough in extending over-sight responsibilities with communities. Is it because we're scared of giving power to the people? Yes, there are risks. There are risks that communities will use racial and ethnic criteria in staffing or rewarding performance. Yes, there are risks that parents often do not have the information or expertise to make some decisions about what is likely to yield better school results.

However, the evidence from this HSRC research shows that in almost all cases, because it is about their own children's education, they take wise, sober decisions, free of such prejudice. While communities are not homogenous, they constitute vibrant, living entities with a high level of organisation. It is up to the institutional and legal framework to provide the space and guidance for communities to become positive influences over the performance of schools. In many cases, we have been too coy about providing the institutional space for people's power to prevail.

The Finance Minister from the state of Kerala in India, Dr Thomas

Isaac, visited the National Treasury recently. As you might know, the state of Kerala is run by the Communist Party and has particularly good educational and health outcomes.

When he was asked about what drove these sterling performances, he replied that in Kerala, when the teacher or nurse does not pitch up at work for a few days, the community will march to the village council and the village council has to report on why the teacher or nurse is not in attendance.

He is immensely proud of the quality of public services in Kerala, delivered for a small fraction of what we spend: teachers, for example earn around $200 per month, roughly one-fifth of what teachers in South Africa have as a starting salary.

In neighbouring Tamil Nadu, if the teacher or nurse does not pitch up, no one bothers. I do not have to tell you about the education or health outcomes in the neighbouring state. When the minister was asked what single factor contributed towards good public services, he said, "we have a robust democracy where people shout loudly and they are heard".

Another example of where the contribution of people has made a difference is in policing. Where community police forums are encouraged and supported by the local police station, they have been invaluable allies in the fight against crime. In public statements, government often makes the call that crime cannot be beaten without solid partnerships with communities. There is clear evidence that the development of trust between the police and communities is a critical element of an effective strategy to reduce crime.

In Naledi in Soweto and in Parkmore in Johannesburg, community police forums have made a positive impact on the work of the police and have contributed both to better relationships with communities and in the reduction in crime levels. Yet there are many communities where people know exactly who the criminals are but they distrust the police to deal with the problem.

However, in policing too we have not fully embraced more democratic forms of governance. There are still too many police stations that give lip service to the notion of community police forums, too many station commanders who would prefer to do without the prying eyes of local residents. We cannot divorce the notion of better public services from the notion of empowering communities. Empowerment is about holding government accountable; it is about making government more responsive and about taking responsibilities for the performance of public services.

When we reminisce about the 1970s and the 1980s, we often remember the mass protests, the community mobilisation, the active involvement of communities in solving their own problems. How did these things occur? Who were the catalysts? Communities did not suddenly wake up and start protesting. No, they were organised by groups of young activists, mostly students.

Thousands of people visited literally millions of homes and spent time talking to families about their issues, their problems and about solutions. The Black Consciousness Movement of the 1970s raised the consciousness of society after the lull of the 1960s, following the banning and imprisonment of many leaders. The United Democratic Front of the 1980s built on top of that a culture of broad participation with the community, including door-to-door work. Politics and revolution were talked about in the homes of the oppressed, in our churches, our schools and universities, on our sports fields, on trains, buses and taxis, not just in town halls.

Where have all the activists gone? What do the young people who are politically astute and socially aware do these days? Who is doing the mobilising? Who are the catalysts for social transformation?

Returning to the issue of economic empowerment, we must ask ourselves the honest but difficult question of whether the Black Economic Empowerment model that we've adopted is meeting both the objectives set out or the aspirations of our people.

Biko, in a paper entitled, "We Blacks", writes, "material want is bad enough but coupled with spiritual poverty, it kills". As early at the mid-1970s, Biko foresaw the effect of this spiritual poverty. He did not mean this in a religious sense. Instead, he was referring to a lack of values, the absence of consciousness and poor understanding. The combined effect is what we today call crass consumerism.

This is an appropriate point to move to the final part of my talk: the construction of a social compact for development. A social compact is not a new concept, yet we've failed to grasp its meaning. At the heart of a social compact is the sense that citizenship is stewardship. A social compact requires society to set out the roles, rights and responsibilities of each element of society; government, business, labour and even the media have a role to play in this regard.

I stress, a social compact is about rights and responsibilities. However, in defining these roles and responsibilities, the primary question must be about the values that a society embraces. These values must have at their core the principles of people-centred development, of freedom, of conscientisation, of mobilisation and of high-energy democracy.

Government has a clear role to play in redistributing opportunities to the most vulnerable. Government has the right to expect from its citizens, both corporate and private, that they pay their taxes, that they abide by the laws of the country in letter and spirit and that all contribute towards development, in the spirit of our Constitution.

Similarly, government has a responsibility to ensure that the quality of public services improves, that we take clear measures to protect citizens, that we spend the public's money wisely, that we clamp down on corruption and patronage, that we employ the best people for the job and that we involve local communities in the improvement of their lives.

Government has the right to intervene to try to correct market failures as efficiently as possible. We have the responsibility to listen to citizens, to create the legal environment for citizens to contribute towards better schooling, better policing and better health care.

Business has the right to invest where they see an opportunity and they have the right to make profits. They have the right to be treated fairly, to be given opportunities free of the obligations of patronage. They have the right for their property rights to be protected and to be treated fairly in matters of taxation. They also have responsibilities; to train their staff, to expand the pool of skilled people and to ensure adequate opportunities for black people and women.

We need elites that plough back, not elites that plunder. We need a business community that balances their freedom to make profits with an understanding of the distorted history of accumulation in our country. We need a private sector that is prepared to be a partner in development; yes, looking for opportunities to make money, but recognising the bigger picture that a stable society is better for growth than a society wracked by social strife.

We also need a private sector that recognises that the present concentration of the economy is not necessarily good for growth and long-term development. This is a difficult situation for business to manage because it is not intuitive to business that long-term growth and prosperity requires a different organisation of ownership. We expect business to take tougher measures to curb anti-competitive practices, to ensure proper governance and over-sight of listed companies and to think consciously about tomorrow, not just today.

Roberto Unger uses a wonderful phrase. He says, "Capitalism must be imposed on the capitalists."[9] Organised labour plays a critical role in the economy and in the delivery of public services. We have a labour regime where the rights of workers are protected, where collective bargaining is entrenched, where, through National Economic Development and Labour Council (NEDLAC), labour plays a role in the development and formulation of policy.

We also need a labour movement that recognises that they have responsibilities too. Expanding employment is a critical requirement in our country and our labour movement has to recognise that there is sometimes a trade-off between the level of wages and the number of people employed.

We need a labour movement that openly condemns its members if they are not teaching the requisite hours, or if they arrive late at school. The labour movement must become a partner in the construction of a state that delivers better services to people.

Communities and community organisations must become the lifeblood of a high-energy democracy as they too have rights and responsibilities. To repeat the lesson from Biko's writings, they cannot be passive recipients of development. Communities were the mainstay of the resistance against apartheid; it was also, incidentally, the object of the black community programmes, undertaken by the Black People's Convention.

When we look back on the uprising at any point in its history, whether it be the defiance campaign of the 1950s, the resistance to pass laws or the roll-out of the M Plan in the 1960s, the BPC programmes of the late 1960s or early 1970s, the support for the student uprising in 1976 and beyond, or whether we are exploring the state of organisation that gave birth to the United Democratic Front (UDF) in 1983 or spawned by UDF activities, the focus has always been on organised communities.

Forget any idea that one fine day in 1985, or whenever, communities across the length and breadth of South Africa suddenly rose up, encouraged to do so by some prophet, perhaps even by a contemporary Nongqawuse, and in the consequence President de Klerk delivered democracy.

Organised communities were truly organised; they were mobilised by the hard work of activists trudging through streets in all weather to talk to people about their lives. This action was first-level conscientisation. Ordinary people thus persuaded would then attend meetings, in order to commune. Frequently people thereafter took responsibility for convening whether it was a street committee, parents' committee, an anti-crime forum, or even a ministers' fraternal. The spark, the initial action, was lit by the activists, mainly students who would undertake such provocative activities after campus.

What we have illustrated is that democracy is now begging for organised communities to fulfil their responsibilities. Democracy is crying out for School Governing Bodies in those areas where the poor have no option but to send their children to the local schools; democracy is pleading with us to improve on the lives of the poor by removing the scourge of crime by holding police locally accountable; democracy is imploring us to give our youth a chance by the organisation of amateur sports codes in townships across the country; she is demanding that we collaborate to ensure that there is value for money in all public services. Democracy understands her origins and her history; she knows that she is the product of high-level sacrifice.

A social compact requires each of us to put our narrow interests aside in the interests of long-term growth and development. It requires hard work, the construction of careful compromises and trade-offs aimed at ending the narrow insider-outsider divide. The cost of failure is high. The cost of failure is that we will continue to lose skills, we will continue to battle with high unemployment and public services will remain poor for the majority of our people. We will continue to see sporadic outbursts of violence. Most importantly, any vision of a better life for all would become a distant dream.

Do we have the leaders in government, in business and in the labour movement to take some of these bold decisions, to confront the difficult trade-offs in the interest of our country? Or are we going to continue to put short-term gain at the expense of longer-term development? I am an optimist and I do believe that South Africa has the leaders to confront these difficult issues, to draw on the inspiration of Biko; to give people-centred democracy a chance to work.

In conclusion let me repeat the lesson that Biko taught us. Democracy is something to fight for, constantly. Development is not something handed out at the welfare office. It is a conscious process of building capabilities, giving communities power to change their lives, empowering young women and men to make a contribution to our beautiful country.

At the root of Biko's teachings and the thread that runs through the references from Marx and Unger is the concept of consciousness, the deep understanding of the self-worth of people and the power of communities. The poor must be given the power to change their lives. Biko's vision of an energised democracy is only possible if we think about empowerment differently. An energised democracy is only possible if we have it within ourselves to construct a social compact that puts our long-term interests above short-term gain. An energised democracy is one where each element – business, labour, government and communities – balance their rights with their responsibilities.

This moment could define our collective future. Let us utilise it for a national catharsis. Let us work together as advised by Unger who writes, "Social solidarity must rest (instead) on the sole secure basis it can have,:direct responsibility of people for one another. Such responsibility can be realised through the principle that every able-bodied adult holds a position within a caring economy, the part of the economy in which people care for one another as well as within the production system."[10]

To dare any less would be to abandon the vision of leaders in the mould of Steve Bantu Biko.

Thank you.

Notes

1. Karl Marx. 1979 [1859]. *A Contribution to the Critique of Political Economy*. London: Lightning Source Inc.
2. Roberto Unger. 2005. *What should the Left Propose?* New York: Verso, p. 3.
3. Steve Biko. 2004 [1978]. *I Write What I Like*. Johannesburg: Picador Africa, p. 96.
4. Biko, *I Write What I Like*, p. 96.
5. Unger, *What should the Left Propose?*
6. Unger, *What should the Left Propose?*
7. Zakes Mda. "Biko's Children". See Chapter 2 of this book, pp. 21–22.
8. Statement of the National Executive Committee of the African National Congress on the occasion of the 96th Anniversary of the ANC. 8 January 2008. See www.anc.org.za/show.php?doc=ancdocs/history/jan8-08.html (accessed 11 June 2009).
9. Unger, *What should the Left Propose?*
10. Unger, *What should the Left Propose?*

Special Acknowledgements

The Steve Biko Foundation would like to say a special thanks to the institutions and individuals whose partnership has made the Steve Biko Memorial Lecture possible. In particular:

- The University of Cape Town, which has served as the co-host of the lecture since its inception, extending both financial and human resources;
- The South African Broadcasting Corporation, which is our broadcast partner in this initiative, ensuring that women and men in 47 African nations are able to share in this legacy; and
- The illustrious leaders whose contributions are chronicled within these pages.

The Foundation would also like to thank the National Heritage Council, whose generous support has made this publication possible.